Microsoft SharePoint

Bible

1

Microsoft SharePoint

Bible

By

Jason Taylor

2

3

TABLE OF CONTENTS

4

6

7

8

9

10

11

12

INTRODUCTION

The need to exchange information within a business or organization is one of the main justifications for utilizing SharePoint. The most popular sharing techniques are as follows:

- Either upload an existing document to the SharePoint site or create a new one right there.
- Add information to a SharePoint list, such as a calendar or a list of team tasks.
- Utilize the Newsfeed located on the SharePoint team site's main page. You can submit an image, tag someone, like or respond to an existing entry, or create a new one.
- Add or modify pages in SharePoint. You may add tables, app components, and web components to your pages, as well as text, photos, links, and videos.

Welcome to the world of SharePoint! In today's fast-paced digital landscape, organizations are increasingly seeking robust solutions to enhance collaboration, streamline workflows, and manage information effectively. SharePoint, a powerful platform developed by Microsoft, has emerged as a leading tool that meets these demands, offering a versatile

13

environment for document management, project collaboration, and information sharing.

This tutorial book is designed to be your comprehensive guide to SharePoint, whether you are a beginner eager to understand the basics or an experienced user looking to deepen your expertise. As we explore the myriad features of SharePoint, you will learn how to harness its capabilities to foster teamwork, improve efficiency, and support your organization's goals.

UNDERSTANDING SHAREPOINT

At its core, SharePoint is a web-based platform that provides a centralized location for storing, organizing, sharing, and accessing information. It enables teams to collaborate seamlessly by offering tools for document management, version control, and real-time editing. SharePoint is not just a document repository; it's a complete ecosystem that supports project management, workflow automation, and business intelligence.

The flexibility of SharePoint allows organizations to tailor their sites according to their unique needs. Whether you're creating a simple team site for a small project or a complex intranet for a large enterprise, SharePoint can adapt to fit your requirements. This versatility makes it an invaluable

14

asset across various industries, from education and healthcare to finance and manufacturing.

PURPOSE OF THIS BOOK

The purpose of this book is to provide a structured and in-depth exploration of SharePoint. Each chapter is designed to build upon the previous one, guiding you through the platform's functionalities while providing practical examples and hands-on exercises. By the end of this tutorial, you will have the skills needed to create, manage, and optimize SharePoint sites effectively.

WHAT YOU WILL LEARN

Throughout this book, you will cover a wide range of topics, including:

Getting Started with SharePoint: We will begin with the fundamentals, guiding you through the process of setting up your SharePoint environment and navigating its interface.

Site Management: You will learn how to create and manage sites, including customizing site layouts, adding web parts, and configuring site settings to enhance user experience.

Document Libraries and Lists: Discover how to create and manage document libraries and lists, implement version

15

control, and utilize metadata for better organization and retrieval of information.

Collaboration Tools: Explore the various collaboration features available in SharePoint, including co-authoring documents, using discussion boards, and integrating with Microsoft Teams for enhanced communication.

Workflows and Automation: Understand how to automate processes using Power Automate, allowing you to streamline repetitive tasks and improve productivity.

Security and Compliance: Learn how to manage permissions effectively, ensuring that sensitive information is protected while still promoting collaboration within your team.

Customization and Development: For those looking to extend SharePoint's capabilities, we will touch upon customization options and introduce you to SharePoint Framework (SPFx) for building custom applications.

WHO SHOULD READ THIS BOOK

This book is intended for a diverse audience. Whether you are a project manager, IT professional, business analyst, or an end-user looking to improve your skills, you will find valuable insights and practical guidance throughout. No

16

prior experience with SharePoint is necessary; however, a basic understanding of web technologies and office productivity tools will be beneficial.

THE IMPORTANCE OF CONTINUOUS LEARNING

As you embark on this learning journey, it's important to remember that SharePoint is a continually evolving platform. Microsoft regularly updates SharePoint with new features and enhancements, making it essential to stay informed about the latest developments. This book aims to provide you not only with foundational knowledge but also the tools to continue learning and adapting as SharePoint grows.

17

CHAPTER ONE
DESIGN

The SharePoint tenancy is at the top of the hierarchy, which is followed by site collections, and the list item is at the bottom. All of the lower levels may be found in each site collection, and elements like as themes, navigation, and permissions can be passed down from upper to lower levels. From the content to the container, we shall examine the many tiers from the bottom up.

APPLICATIONS

Every SharePoint application is housed inside a website. They can fall into one of three categories:

- **Lists**: A list and an Excel table are extremely similar. It includes things like contacts in a contact list, tasks in a tasks list, and appointments in a calendar list. Another option is to make your own unique list, like a Cost Center list. There are numerous parameters for every list, including which columns, views, and permissions are appropriate for use on that list.

- **Libraries of documents**: A library has most of the same options and capabilities as a list and can perform nearly everything that a list can. What they include is the primary distinction. Libraries hold

18

files; lists contain items. Consult the SharePoint Libraries.

- **Other applications:** These can have a variety of appearances and behaviors. I don't mean other apps when I talk about apps; I mean lists or libraries. Lists, such as calendars and libraries, employ columns to describe the content using keywords and metadata. The lists themselves include views that present the content from multiple perspectives, and the columns can be filtered in a variety of ways.

THE 5000 LIMIT

Because SharePoint does not function effectively when an application contains more than 5000 items, you should avoid making your apps too large. Libraries with more than 5000 items cannot be synchronized with OneDrive for Business, and views cannot display more than 5000 items.

PAGES

The top navigation menu and Quick Launch serve as boundaries for the large area in the center of a SharePoint page. Every page has a unique URL. Application pages and site pages are the two types of pages. Typically, settings control is done through application pages. They come from Microsoft and are completely un-customizable in SharePoint

19

Online. Because site pages are customizable, we will focus primarily on them in this book. The content you put in the center and how you customize it determine how a page of your website looks. Text, photos, videos, and web components (which can show app content) can all be found on site pages. The majority of pages are kept in a library known as **Site Pages**.

SharePoint comes with two types of site pages by default:

- Wiki pages and
- Web part pages

PAGES ON WIKIPEDIA

When you create a new page, it will most typically be a wiki page. Here, you can create different types of Web Parts, add text or links, or directly integrate photos, videos, and other content into the page.

PAGES IN WEB PARTS

Forms and views are stored on web component pages. Though not as freely customizable as wiki pages, they are nevertheless intended to be changed. Rather, it is codified using web component zones that are difficult to modify.

20

HOW TO ADD A PAGE

- To add a new page, click the settings gear and choose "Add a page."
- You can name the page in the window that appears, and the page will be created when you click the Create button.
- To allow for customization, it will launch in edit mode.

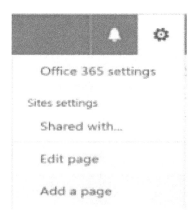

WEBSITES FOR SHAREPOINT

The key component of the SharePoint tenant is the SharePoint sites. Every SharePoint task, including adding content, is completed within the framework of a site. There can only be two items on a site:

- Subsites and

21

- Apps

Every website has a vast array of settings that affect how it functions and appears.

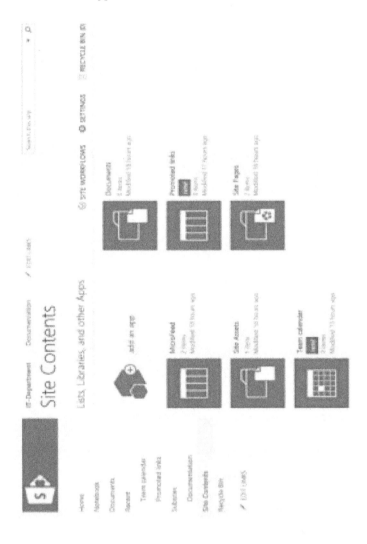

CONTENTS OF THE SITE

- Click the Site Contents link in the Quick Launch box on the left to view a site's entire contents.
- A page with icons and links to all content will open. Take note of the header "Lists, Libraries and other Apps."

CONFIGURING THE SITE

The site's settings can be accessed through the settings gear in the Site Contents and the Right Navigation Bar.

MAKE A NEW WEBSITE

Open the Site Contents of any existing site, then select the "new subsite" link to establish a new SharePoint subsite site. Every site established, with the exception of the site collection root site, has a parent site because all sites are derived from pre-existing sites.

Subsites

⊕ new subsite

This site does not have any subsites.

See Create a Subsite for information on how to create a new site from the Sites Page. There are various types of site

23

templates available when you establish a new website. There are options for the navigation, and you can specify whether the permissions are unique or inherited.

SITE COLLECTION

As the name suggests, a SharePoint site collection is a group of sites. Even though they aren't often called that, site collections form the foundation of a large portion of SharePoint. The term "site" might occasionally genuinely refer to a collection of sites.

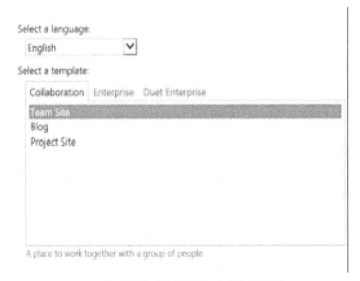

THE ADMIN CENTER FOR SHAREPOINT

The SharePoint Admin Center is where new SharePoint site collections are established, as well as where you can view

24

and access existing site collections and control numerous other SharePoint tenant settings. To access the Office 365 Admin Center, click on the Office 365 Admin tile.

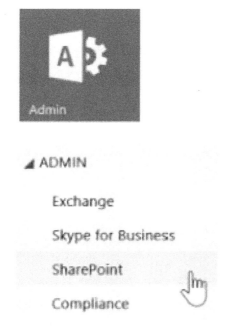

The link to the SharePoint Admin Center is located at the bottom of the Office 365 Admin Center's left panel.

All of the tenant's site collections are visible in the SharePoint admin center. There are linkages to site collections that are automatically generated when SharePoint is installed, even on your first visit to the admin

25

area. You will probably want to return to the SharePoint Admin Center frequently, so it is a good idea to bookmark it in your browser after you have found it.

MAKE A NEW COLLECTION OF SITES

- Select "Private Site Collection" after clicking the "New" button on the ribbon. (The option to establish a public site collection was once accessible, but it is no longer available.)

- A new dialog box for site collection will appear. Create the other parameters you like, then give the new site collection a name. Press OK.

- Although it is typically much faster, SharePoint may take up to 15 minutes to establish the new site collection.

- A root site for the site collection is created by SharePoint during the creation process, and it has the URL "https:// [tenant].sharepoint.com/sites/[site collection name]"

26

CHAPTER TWO

TEAM WEBSITE

The team site is the most popular kind of SharePoint site and is designed for work group collaboration.

THE TEAM SITE BY DEFAULT

Certain SharePoint site collections are pre-made when you purchase an Office 365 subscription that includes SharePoint. The team site collection is the most crucial one and features the following traits:

- The Team Site template serves as its foundation.
- By default, the team site has all of the tenant's users added.
- By default, all users are added with the ability to edit.

It should be noted that this is a very high degree of permission for everyone to possess. The majority of SharePoint administrators would like to alter that. Sharing with the outside world is enabled. **There is no scripting enabled.**

Scripting will be enabled and external sharing will not be enabled by default when you create a new site collection in the SharePoint Admin Center. By default, no users will be added. External sharing can be enabled, but scripting for newly generated site collections cannot be disabled.

GET TO THE TEAM LOCATION

The root site of the default team site collection is accessible to all users via the App Launcher or the Sites button on the Office 365 home page.

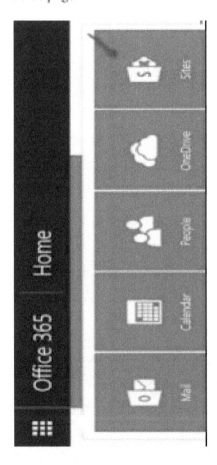

CONTENT BY DEFAULT

The Site Contents are the same for both the root site of the default site collection and any additional subsites you make using the team site template. Two pages—the home page and a page with library instructions within the Site Pages library—are included, along with libraries for Documents and Site Assets. For the Newsfeed that is automatically displayed on the front page, there is also a Microfeed list.

THE MAIN PAGE

The default home page of a SharePoint team site is displayed in the image below. Naturally, it is meant to be tailored to each business, but for the purposes of this discussion, we will use it to go over the various components.

- Refer to the Office 365 Navigation Bar to access the Office 365 area, which is identical to that found in the majority of Office 365 apps. For the SharePoint administrator, there is a significant distinction, though, as the settings gear offers a wide range of options for controlling and altering the SharePoint site. Under that gear, regular users with site editing rights can also add new apps and pages.

- The tabs on the SharePoint ribbon house a number of controls. The tabs and controls within those tabs

29

change based on what you have selected and the
object you are working with, as is always the case
with the Office ribbon. The controls under the PAGE
tab are displayed in the image below.

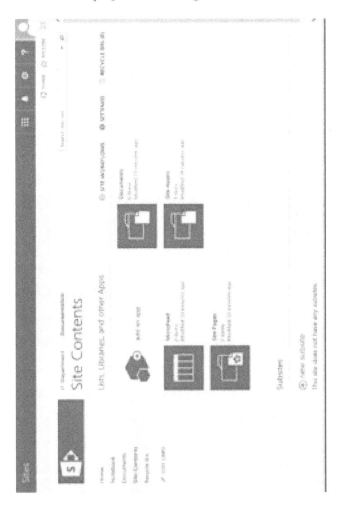

30

- Links to websites within the same site collection are typically displayed in the Top Navigation.

- Links to apps on the current website are typically displayed in the Quick Launch.

- To share websites, use the SHARE command. Although other sites also employ the SHARE command, the team site is rarely used because it is shared by default by all of the tenant's user accounts.

- The FOLLOW command allows any user to follow sites.

- The Sites Page contains a list of all the websites the user has followed.

- To change SharePoint Wiki Pages, use the EDIT command to open them in edit mode. A SAVE command takes the place of the EDIT command when a page is open in edit mode.

- The page without the navigation elements is displayed when the Focus on Content command is used. To display the menu, click the button once more.

- SharePoint uses the Search field for Global Search. The current site is searched by default,

31

but you can filter the search or look through all of the tenant's material by going to Search.

- If you're new to SharePoint, the Get Started tiles include links that can be helpful. After some time, when the team site needs to be modified, these tiles are frequently taken down.

- Clicking REMOVE THIS makes it simple to get rid of them. See Promoted Links for information on how to make your own link tiles.

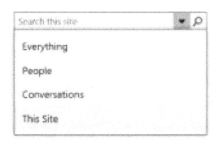

- The Newsfeed is designed to facilitate the exchange of ideas and information among team site users. In their profile, each user can specify their own Newsfeed preferences. See Add Links to a Newsfeed as well.

- Although SharePoint stores various file types in document libraries, an app part can also be used

32

to show the content of those libraries on a page. There is a web component part on your site's main page (Home.aspx) that shows the files in the library of documents. You can upload existing files, generate new ones, and search through them here.

THE GALLERIES FOR SHAREPOINT WEB DESIGNERS

You may manage reusable elements in a SharePoint site collection, such as content types, site columns, and solutions, in the SharePoint Web Designer Galleries. The SharePoint Web Designer Galleries will be shown in the Site settings by default when you manually build a new site. However, the SharePoint Web Designer Galleries are not displayed on the initial, automatically generated team site, which could potentially pose issues for SharePoint administrators.

In the default team site's site settings, enable the SharePoint Web Designer Galleries group as follows:

- Launch the Admin Center for SharePoint.
- Select "settings" from the panel on the left.
- Locate the Custom Script area by scrolling down.

33

- Turn on the "Allow users to run custom script on self-service created sites" radio button.

NAVIGATION

The structure and manipulation of the SharePoint navigation must be understood by SharePoint administrators. Two navigation panels are present on the majority of SharePoint pages. Although you are free to include any links in both panels, I advise using them in distinct ways. While other links that users may not use frequently are located at the top of the page, it is simpler for consumers to understand that apps on the same website are located in the left panel.

NAVIGATION AT THE TOP

The Top or Global Navigation is the name of the navigation banner that appears at the top of the page. Links to other sites within the same site collection are often displayed, but you are free to add any links you like, including links to external information that is not hosted by your SharePoint tenancy.

QUICK LAUNCH

The Quick Launch or Current Navigation is the name of the navigation panel on the left side of the page. Usually, it displays links to information or apps on the current website.

34

Home

Notebook

Documents

Site Contents

 EDIT LINKS

LINKS THAT ARE INHERITED

A new website may inherit the parent site's top navigation when it is created. To accomplish this, click the radio button in the Site Settings:

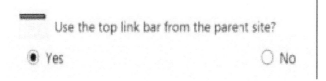
Use the top link bar from the parent site?

◉ Yes   ○ No

MODIFY LINKS

To access the navigation panels in edit mode, click EDIT LINKS. The Quick Launch functions similarly to the top navigation, as seen in the figure below.

- To remove a link, use the X icon. To conceal a link, use the eye icon.

35

- Use drag and drop to rearrange the links.
- Click the +link symbol to add new links. In the window that appears, enter the path or paste the display text for the new link.
- In edit mode, add links to the Quick Launch by dragging the desired program into the Quick Launch from Site Contents.
- When you're finished, save the modifications.

Look and Feel
Title, description, and logo
Quick launch
Top link bar
Navigation Elements
Change the look

From the Site Settings, you can also change the navigation. Although there are links to edit pages for both navigation panels in the Look and Feel group, further customization is not possible here. All you can do is add, remove, and rearrange links.

36

CHAPTER THREE

THE HIERARCHY OF NAVIGATION

To establish a hierarchy, you can drag connections beneath one another. Make a link without a route and drag other links underneath it to create a heading. The Department caption is not linked in the picture below.

Compared to before you activated the SharePoint Server Publishing Infrastructure, you will have additional navigation options when you click on the new Navigation link. The new Navigation settings page includes the box below.

PERMISSION

37

If you are comfortable with the default settings, using SharePoint permissions is fairly simple. For a small team, it might work, but SharePoint permissions become more complicated if you want more control over what users can see and do. But you can also profit from the advantages that come with knowing how SharePoint permissions operate.

LEVELS OF PERMISSION

In reality, the permission levels are collections of related permissions. You don't need to grant each of these four rights independently, for instance, if you wish to grant a user the ability to view, add, update, and remove documents and list items but nothing else. Alternatively, you might set this user's permission to the pre-established "Contribute" level. Site Settings > People and Groups > Permission levels > the Permission Levels button on the ribbon is where you may access the built-in permission levels.

You can see what the various levels allow users to perform on the Permission Levels page. Although editing these settings is feasible, I advise against it. Making your own Custom Permission Levels is safer. Levels on this page can also be removed, but before you do so, consider your options

38

carefully and test three times in a collection of non-production sites!

Permissions · Permission Levels ⊙

Add a Permission Level | X Delete Selected Permission Levels

Permission Level	Description
Full Control	Has full control.
Design	Can view, add, update, delete, approve, and customize.
Edit	Can add, edit and delete lists; can view, add, update and delete list items and documents.
Contribute	Can view, add, update, and delete list items and documents.
Read	Can view pages and list items and download documents.
Limited Access	Can view specific lists, document libraries, list items, folders, or documents when given permissions.
View Only	Can view pages, list items, and documents. Document types with server side file handlers can be viewed in the browser but not downloaded.
Approve	Can edit and approve pages, list items, and documents.
Manage Hierarchy	Can create sites and edit pages, list items, and documents.
Restricted Read	Can view pages and documents, but cannot view historical versions or user permissions.
Restricted Interfaces for Translation	Can open lists and folders, and use remote interfaces.

39

PERMISSION LEVEL BY DEFAULT

All users in SharePoint Online have the default privilege level set to Edit. This implies that users can add, edit, and remove lists and libraries, as well as create, edit, and remove columns and public views, in addition to viewing, adding, updating, and deleting documents and list items by default. This is a high level, in my opinion, but as long as you are aware of it, there is no issue, and you are free to choose whether to modify or maintain it.

LEVEL OF CUSTOM PERMISSION

You can just construct your own permission level if none of the pre-defined ones work. On the Permission Levels page, click "Add a Permission Level." A new page will open with options for what the new permission level should permit. "Add but not delete" is one of these often-requested access levels.

INHERITANCE

Under the site collection root site level, SharePoint sites, applications, and so forth automatically inherit the same permissions as the higher level. As a result, sites are granted the same permissions as site collections, lists are granted site permissions, and items are granted list permissions.

40

- Site collections
  - Sites
    - Lists and Libraries
      - Items

Therefore, if you don't break the inheritance, users who have edit permission on a site by default also have edit permission on all of its lists and, if you don't break the inheritance, edit permission on every item in each list!

User Permissions:

   ○ Use same permissions as parent site

   ◉ Use unique permissions

BREACK THE INHERITANCE

Breaking the inheritance is not hard. It is possible to choose a different radio button than the default one when creating a new website. All levels down to the item level can have their inheritance broken, but not the column level. A permissions page appears when you select the radio button for unique permissions:

41

- There is no such option when creating an application or a page. Rather, you must launch the application or website and halt the inheritance.
- Locate the Shared With command and access the advanced options to halt the inheritance of existing permissions. It is located on the LIBRARY tab of the ribbon for libraries.
- Click on the ellipses and select Shared With under Advanced to prevent file and list item inheritance.
- To see the screen where you can cease inheriting in any scenario, click ADVANCED. To stop inheriting permissions, click on it.

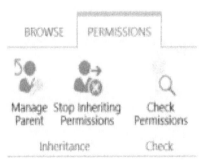

- In order to grant new permissions, the ribbon will now alter.
- To return to the inherited permission levels, click "Delete unique permissions."

42

- Keep in mind that a page is still a file and an object, so you would take the same actions as before if you wanted to give a page special access.

GROUPS WITH PERMISSION

For better permission management, I propose you to form Office 365 security groups of users who should have the same access level. For instance, when you wish to grant users access to many site collections, this makes maintenance easier. Adding an Office 365 security group is far faster than adding each user one at a time. Three SharePoint Groups are automatically present on a team site: Owners, Members, and Visitors.

You can make your own permission groups, but you can also add new users or Office 365 security groups to these groups.

BROWSE	PERMISSIONS			
Delete unique permissions	Grant Permissions	Edit User Permissions	Remove User Permissions	Check Permissions
Inheritance	Grant		Modify	Check

43

MAKE A NEW GROUP OF PERMISSIONS

Office 365 security groups are created via the Office 365 Admin Center, which is also where all user management is done.

- Launch the Admin Center for Office 365.

- Select GROUPS from the panel on the left.

- Press the plus symbol.

- Click the radio button for the Security group. Press the Next button.

- Click Next after giving the group a name and a description.

- SharePoint will provide you with suggestions as soon as you begin typing the name of the person you wish to add to the group. Choose the appropriate recommendation. Proceed to the following individual. Select "Add Members."

- Choose the group from the list of groups under the plus symbol to change its members or remove it altogether. You can now edit or remove the group using the panel that appears.

44

Security group

Use to assign SharePoint permissions

3 members

✏ EDIT MEMBERS　　🗑 DELETE GROUP

INFORMATION RIGHTS MANAGEMENT

The weakest security points in an organization's security system are frequently files and emails. When unprotected documents are shared on memory sticks or emailed as email attachments, aggressors can access them. Similarly, unprotected emails pose a risk since they can be shared outside the company. Information Rights Management, or IRM, is necessary for this reason. You can restrict what users can do with emails and files that have been downloaded from SharePoint libraries if you enable IRM in Office 365. For instance, users may be able to browse files but not print or copy them thanks to the IRM settings.

Since Office 365 makes it easier to establish IRM than on-premise installations, it is a key selling feature for Office 365. Here, I'll go over how to activate Office 365's basic IRM and how to activate IRM in a SharePoint document

45

Jason Taylor

library.

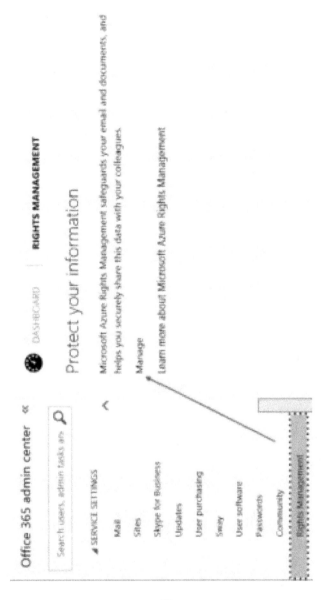

HOW TO TURN ON OFFICE 365'S BASIC INFORMATION RIGHTS MANAGEMENT

IRM must be enabled in the Office 365 Admin Center before it can be enabled in SharePoint.

- Launch the Admin Center for Office 365.
- Select the "Rights Management" tab under SERVICE SETTINGS.
- Select the Manage hyperlink.
- To activate Basic IRM, click the first Activate button.

rights management

ⓘ Rights Management is not activated

Rights Management safeguards your email and documents, and helps
you securely share this data with your colleagues.

To enable Rights Management, click activate.

- Verify that it is activated.

47

CHAPTER FOUR

HOW TO ACTIVATE SHAREPOINT'S BASIC INFORMATION RIGHTS MANAGEMENT

You can activate IRM for SharePoint once the tenant's IRM has been activated.

- Launch the Admin Center for SharePoint.
- In the left panel, click the "settings" link.
- Select the radio option labeled "Use the IRM service specified in your configuration" under Information Rights Management (IRM).
- Select the button to Refresh IRM Settings.

HOW TO GIVE A LIBRARY ACCESS TO BASIC INFORMATION RIGHTS MANAGEMENT

You can enable IRM for a document library after you've enabled it for the tenant and SharePoint:

- Launch the library and SharePoint site where you wish to use IRM as such.
- Access the Library Preferences.
- In the Permissions and Management group, select the Information Rights Management link.
- Check the option to restrict download permissions.
- Type a description and a title.

48

Settings · Information Rights Management Settings

Information Rights Management (IRM)

IRM helps protect sensitive files from being removed or distributed without permission once they have been downloaded from this library.

☑ Restrict permissions on this library on download
Create a permission policy title

Add a permission policy description

How do I...

Set additional IRM library settings
This section provides additional settings that control the library behavior.

☐ Do not allow users to upload documents that do not support IRM
☐ Stop restricting access to the library at
☐ Prevent opening documents in the browser for this Document Library

Configure document access rights
This section controls document access rights (for viewers) after the document is downloaded from this library; it can only restrict rights to the default. Granting these rights below is reducing the bar for accessing the unrestricted vault.

☐ Allow viewers to print
☐ Allow viewers to run script and screen reader to function on downloaded documents
☐ Allow viewers to write on a copy of the downloaded document
☐ After download, document access rights will expire after these number of days (1-365)

Set group protection and credentials interval
Use the settings in this section to control the caching policy of the license that opens the document that opens the document will use and to allow sharing the downloaded document with users that belong to a specified group.

☐ Users must verify their credentials using this interval (days)
☐ Allow group protection. Default group.
Enter a name or email address.

49

Press the SHOW OPTIONS button.

- Select the limits you wish to impose by checking the boxes.

SHAREPOINT APPLICATIONS

Lists or applications can be used to store and exchange material within websites. Examples of applications include calendars, contact lists, picture libraries, and document libraries. All app kinds have certain characteristics. You should utilize them for information that needs to be shared, not for personal information, as they are all shared among a group of individuals. (After all, that is SharePoint's primary function.)

ADVANTAGES

A spreadsheet or database table is comparable to a SharePoint application. Each row is referred to as a list item, and data is dispersed in rows. There are multiple columns in each row, or item, where you can enter metadata — descriptive information about the thing. The advantages of SharePoint apps are numerous. An excellent overview of data is provided by SharePoint apps.

To locate information, utilize the robust SharePoint Search function.

50

You can view previous iterations of each item and the specific changes made in each version using the SharePoint Versioning feature. Items can be sorted and filtered so that you can examine the data in various ways. To permanently filter or show items in a SharePoint list in a specific manner, you can construct several Views. You can use sum, average, and other metrics to summarize the values of your items using the Totals feature. SharePoint data can be exported and connected to Outlook, Excel, Access, Visio, and Project. Singular list items can have their permissions configured so that only specific individuals can see them. When items are added or modified to the list, you can allow SharePoint to notify you.

LIST SETTINGS

Every application has a settings page with a wide variety of settings, such as those for views, columns, and permissions. The LIST tab in the ribbon has the List Settings button. The Library Settings button is located under the LIBRARY tab in libraries, and the CALENDAR tab is found in calendars.

51

The Site Contents can also be used to access the list settings. A SETTINGS link will appear when you click on the ellipsis at the list you wish to utilize. Depending on the type of app, the settings pages vary slightly, but they all offer a wide range of customization choices for the list.

SEARCH

SharePoint has multiple methods for searching through all or a portion of the content in lists, sites, or collections. We'll examine the two search fields now.

There are two distinct search fields for local and global searches in SharePoint lists and libraries. Only the global search is available for the calendar and survey lists.

52

Permissions filter the results when you use SharePoint Search. As a result, only results that each user is permitted to view will be displayed.

LOCAL LOOKUP

Lists and libraries have a local search box. SharePoint searches the current list or library when you type something into the local search field and hit Enter.

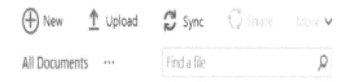

WORLDWIDE SEARCH

Regardless of where you are in SharePoint—a website or a specific app—the global search field at the top right of the screen is meant to always be available. SharePoint automatically searches the current site when you type something into the global search field. The global search, however, offers more choices.

The whole SharePoint tenant is searched by the search engine when you use the global search with the Everything, People, and Conversations options. The results are shown on

53

a tenant's Search Center page. The Search Center's default URL is /search/.

A search results page for the current site will display the search results when you perform the global search with the default choice, This Site.

ADD AN APP

To create a new application, use the "add an app" command. In addition to creating your own templates (see Save the List as a Template), SharePoint Online provides a number of templates on which you can build a new application. The SharePoint site where you create each new application will house it.

- Select Add an app after opening the settings gear.

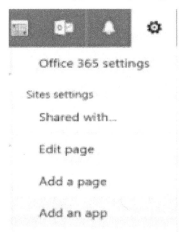

Office 365 settings

Sites settings

Shared with...

Edit page

Add a page

Add an app

54

- Another option is to click on "add an app" after opening the Site Contents library from the Quick Launch or Settings gear.

- Either choose the Custom List or locate the list app that most closely resembles the list you wish to build. To create the new app, click the icon.
- Click Create after giving the list a name. You can access a few additional settings by clicking on the Advanced Options link.

DISPLAY MODES FOR VIEW

Both Standard and Quick Edit modes are available for displaying lists and libraries. The LIST or LIBRARY tab allows you to modify the view display mode. We can tell that this screenshot was taken from a list in Standard view mode because the View button is greyed out in the image below. When the list is displayed in Quick Edit mode or when

55

switching to the Edit more option is not feasible for any other reason, the Quick Edit button is grayed out. Although you can create new Datasheet/Edit views in a calendar list, calendars do not have an edit option in the calendar views.

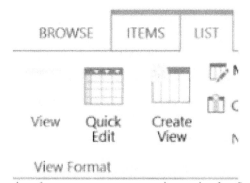

There is a button to create new items in the Standard view display mode.

 New

You may view options for what to do with each item by clicking on the ellipsis (…) that appears next to it. When you left or right-click on the ellipsis in lists, the dropdown menu appears. When you right-click on a library, the option dropdown is shown. Information about the file will appear if you left-click on the ellipsis.

56

Additionally, the information window features an ellipsis to the right of the file name that provides the same menu options as a left-click.

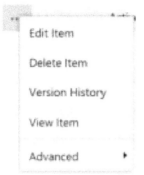

QUICK EDIT

You can make changes directly in the cells and add new rows and List Columns while an application is in Quick Edit mode, which makes it resemble a spreadsheet. As you proceed to the following row, your modifications are saved. For anyone familiar with working with Excel lists, the Quick Edit, or Datasheet, view is incredibly popular and effective. Some fill commands and copy and paste functions are functional in this view.

57

HOW TO LAUNCH THE APPLICATION IN EDIT MODE

- Click the Quick Edit button on the ribbon LIST/LIBRARY tab to open an application in edit mode from Standard view mode.
- You can also select the "edit" link located to the right of the new item link in lists.

ADD AN ITEM

Depending on the type of app and the view display mode you are using, there are multiple ways to create a new item in an app.

The ITEMS/FILES/EVENTS tab has a New button in the left corner for all types of apps and display modes.

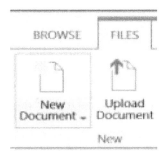

NEW ITEM ON THE LIST

Depending on the view display style, there are two more ways to create new list items.

58

STANDARD MODE NEW LIST ITEM

There is a "+new item" link at the top of lists. To open the new item form, click on it.

QUICK EDIT MODE FOR A NEW LIST ITEM

You can input or choose data for each column in the blank row at the bottom of lists in edit mode.

CHAPTER FIVE

A NEW LIBRARY FILE

Refer to Add Content to Document Libraries for information on how to create new files in document libraries and upload files that already exist elsewhere.

A NEW EVENT ON THE CALENDAR

When you move the mouse pointer over a calendar date in the Month view or over an hour part in the Week and Day views, a "+ Add" option appears, which can be used to add new calendar events.

EDIT THE ITEM

Information is added in a form when calendar events and list items are created. Simply reopen these forms to make changes. To open the form in edit mode, click the Edit Item/Edit Event button either in the open item/event or beneath the ITEMS/EVENTS tab on the ribbon.

You can alternatively open the entire list in edit mode and

60

modify the cell values, or you can right-click on the ellipsis at the item you wish to modify and choose Properties.

MODIFY THE PROPERTIES OF THE FILE

Library documents contain properties form for metadata, which you must automatically open and fill out in order to add metadata to files.

- Click on Edit Properties under the ribbon's FILES tab after selecting the file to open the properties window.

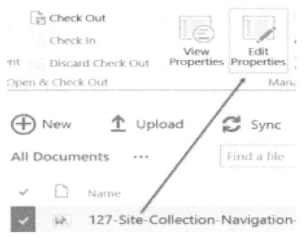

61

Jason Taylor

COLUMNS

Each list item's contents are stored in various types of columns. Columns come in a variety of forms and function differently. One line of text is the default column type, but you have additional choices when creating or editing a column:

- Even while each field does not need to be filled out for every item in the list, they are often the same for every item (unless you use multiple content types; see Create a Content Type Form).

The type of information in this column is:

- ● Single line of text
- ○ Multiple lines of text
- ○ Choice (menu to choose from)
- ○ Number (1, 1.0, 100)
- ○ Currency ($, ¥, €)
- ○ Date and Time
- ○ Lookup (information already on this site)
- ○ Yes/No (check box)
- ○ Person or Group
- ○ Hyperlink or Picture
- ○ Calculated (calculation based on other columns)
- ○ Task Outcome
- ○ External Data
- ○ Managed Metadata

62

- The columns appear as fields when you enter the data using the list item form. As a result, fields are another name for SharePoint list columns. Metadata is a common term used to describe the data in the list columns.

ESTABLISH A COLUMN

Site columns and list columns are two separate types of columns that you should be aware of when you add new columns to your lists. From the List Settings, both can be added. There are three options for adding a new list column under the titles of the current columns:

- Use site columns as much as you can, in my opinion. For really long lists (more than 5000 items), index-columns can be useful, but I suggest archiving things or splitting lists instead of allowing them to get that enormous.

  - Create column

  - Add from existing site columns

  - Indexed columns

63

COLUMNS IN THE LIST

You can create a list column that is only accessible for the current list by selecting the first option in the settings, Create column, which opens a Create Column dialog.

- Choose the column type and give it a name.
- Then, based on the list type you chose, you will have several possibilities.

There are two additional methods for creating list columns:

- Using the LIST/LIBRARY/CALENDAR tab's Create column button. You'll be sent straight to the Create Column dialog box.
- Click the + symbol after opening the list in Quick Edit mode. You will be taken to the Create Column page if you choose More Column kinds, but you can choose the most popular column kinds immediately.

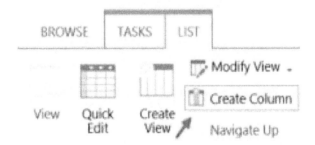

64

COLUMNS ON THE SITE

Multiple apps inside a site collection can be assigned to a site column, which is a reusable column. To create uniformity across lists and libraries, site columns are helpful. To avoid having to generate the site column settings every time, you can use them across lists and libraries. Users can add a site column called Consultants, for instance, to other apps, and it will appear in the entire site collection or even the entire tenant.

Content Types are reusable groups of columns and settings that always use site columns. You will have a wide variety of columns to choose from when you choose the second option for adding a column in the list settings, Add from existing site columns.

65

Although there are several built-in site columns provided by Microsoft, you are free to build your own. The Site Settings >Site columns are where this is done:

VIEWS

Every list has the ability to display data in several ways. Unlike a filtered column, a list view is a permanent filter. Every view is a distinct .aspx page that may be edited, linked to, and accessed in a new tab. "All Items" in lists, "All Documents" in libraries, and "All Events" in calendars are the default views that SharePoint created. Day, Week, and Month can be displayed in the All Events view. All things or files are displayed in these simple views.

Views can be classified as either public or personal. Public views are visible to all users, whereas personal views are only visible to the person who created them. The default view, which we are discussing below, is the public view. In a list or library, you can see up to three views above the objects. The links to change the view or create a new one are located behind the ellipsis, which conceals the others.

In order to organize data and build new views that are appropriate for your organization, I advise you to employ columns for pertinent metadata together with meaningful views. In this manner, the data can be manipulated in a

66

variety of ways, and your SharePoint applications will be highly educational. You can make a Views Landing Page if your list or library has a lot of views.

EXAMINE YOUR OPTIONS

Whether you build a completely new view or alter an existing one, the options and choices are essentially the same. You will have access to all the columns, the ability to add or remove columns, the ability to sort, filter, group, and much more on both the Create View and Edit View pages. We'll provide some samples of what you can accomplish below.

Display	Column Name	Position from Left
☑	Title (linked to item with edit menu)	1
☐	App Created By	2
☐	App Modified By	3
☐	Attachments	4
☐	Content Type	5
☐	Created	6
☐	Created By	7
☐	Declared Record	8
☐	Edit (link to edit item)	9
☐	Folder Child Count	10
☐	ID	11
☐	Item Child Count	12
☐	Modified	13
☐	Modified By	14
☐	Title	15
☐	Title (linked to item)	16
☐	Type (icon linked to document)	17
☐	Version	18

67

ADJUST THE PERSPECTIVE

Here's how to begin altering an existing view:

- After the view name or views, click the ellipsis and choose Modify the View.
- On the LIBRARY/LIST/CALENDAR tab, select the Modify View button.
- In the List Settings, select the view name from the list of available views.

MAKE A VIEW

All SharePoint lists, with the exception of the OneDrive for Business default library, allow you to create new views. Use one of the following techniques to begin developing a new view:

- After the view name or names, click the ellipsis and choose Create View.
- On the LIBRARY/LIST/CALENDAR tab, select the Create View button.
- Under the list of existing views in the List Settings, click the Create view link.
- Regardless of the technique you choose, you will be taken to the View Type page, where you may choose the type of library or list you want to build.

68

(Alternatively, you can start with an existing view and make changes to it.)

Settings › View Type ⊚

Choose a view type

Standard View
View data on a Web page. You can choose from a list of display styles.

Calendar View
View data as a daily, weekly, or monthly calendar.

Access View
Start Microsoft Access to create forms and reports that are based on this list.

Start from an existing view

▪ All Documents

Datasheet View
View data in an editable spreadsheet format that is convenient for bulk editing and quick customization.

Gantt View
View list items in a Gantt chart to see a graphical representation of how a team's tasks relate over time.

Custom View in SharePoint Designer
Start SharePoint Designer to create a new view for this list with capabilities such as conditional formatting.

69

The View Options seen above will appear once you have chosen the Standard, Datasheet, or Gantt view. The Access and SharePoint Designer Views launch Access or SharePoint Designer, while the Calendar View opens a page with many options.

THE STANDARD VIEW

If you set a view as the default, all users will arrive at that view first, regardless of how they launch the application, and the view name will appear first in the list of views. On the Create View/Edit View page, select the default box to make a view the default.

If you tick this option for a different view, that view will be used by default. The All documents or All items view will revert to its original default if you simply uncheck the box in the default view.

VIEW IN GROUPS

Start with the Standard view and navigate to the Group By section on the Create View/Edit View page to create a view that groups objects. To enlarge the accordion, click the + symbol. You can choose which columns to group by on the first and second levels here, as well as how the data in those columns should be shown. One possible explanation for not making a grouped view the default is that the Quick Edit mode does not function in grouped views. Not every kind of column may be grouped, so the dropdowns only display columns that are appropriate for grouping.

CHAPTER SIX

THE TOTALS FEATURE

The data in a column can be summed up using the Totals feature. Other values, such as average, maximum, and minimum, can also be computed for number columns using SharePoint Totals. On top of the computed column is the outcome of the calculation. However, in Quick Edit mode, it is not displayed. The Totals feature can also be used to determine how many items of each category are in a column. On the Create/Edit View screen, click the plus symbol after scrolling down to Totals. From the dropdown menu to the right of the column that should contain the Totals, choose the value you wish to compute.

It is necessary to compute the average of the Amount column in the image below. Keep in mind that not all column types can use the totals feature in the same way. It performs best on columns that contain numbers and money, less well on columns that contain text, and not at all on columns that contain calculations.

VIEWS THE LANDING PAGE

Only three views can be displayed directly on the page of a SharePoint list. You must click on the ellipsis to access the other perspectives. You can make a landing page that appears

72

when users launch the app if you want to show them a summary of all views. Additional information beyond the visible links to this page can also be added. In order to construct the landing page, you must first create the page with the links and then change the app's links to refer to the new landing page.

- Make a page.
- Add the view links to the newly opened page and save it.

CHANGE THE APP LINK

Make sure that when users launch the app, they are taken to the landing page once it has been established. This implies that you need to modify the Quick Launch link.

- Launch the Site Pages Library after opening the Site Contents.
- Remove the default program link by opening Quick Launch in edit mode.
- Drag the landing page from the Site pages to the location where you would like the Quick Launch to display a link to the landing page.
- Save the modifications. In this manner, when consumers click on the app link, they will be taken to the landing page.

73

- If Drag and drop doesn't always work, create a new link to the Quick Launch by copying the link to the new landing page.
- Another alternative is to click on the navigation option in the Look and Feel group after opening Site Settings.

DELETE

The Quick Edit mode is ideal for deleting many items or files since it allows you to pick multiple rows at once:

- Click on the first cell on the left of the objects you wish to remove while holding down the Ctrl key.
- Use the right-click menu to select Delete.

The Delete option under the **Items/Files/Events** tab can be used to remove a single item, file, or event.

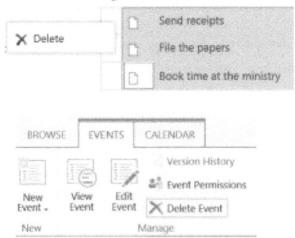

74

You can also click on the ellipsis and choose the Delete option to remove a library file or list item.

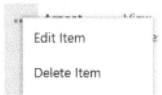

Edit Item

Delete Item

You can click the Delete Item button in the item ribbon to remove a calendar event or an open list item.

Delete
Item

Actions

TEMPLATELY SAVE THE APP

A custom application should be saved as a template if you intend to use it repeatedly. Similar to lists, custom document libraries can be saved as templates.

- Select the "Save list as template" link under the Permissions and Management group in the List Settings.
- Save the template after giving it a name. The template you produced will now be saved as a STP file in the site collection's List Template Gallery.

75

Add an app and choose the template to generate a new list from it.

The template can be uploaded to another site collection. You can download the template file from the List Template Gallery to your computer and then upload it to the List Template Gallery in the site collection where you wish to use it if you want to use an app template for more than just that collection.

When you have the same license, settings, and activated features on the site collections, this works.

- Go to the site collection root site's Site Settings.
- In the Web Designer Galleries group, select the "List templates" option.
- Select the STP file you wish to download from the List Template Gallery.
- Click the upload icon under the FILES tab in the List Template Gallery of the second site collection, then upload the STP file.

Remember to modify any default column values to fit another site collection before you begin utilizing the template in the new site collection.

76

SHAREPOINT CALENDARS

Share event details, such as holidays, vacations, delivery dates, and other information that is relevant to all users with calendar access, such as workgroup members, by using a SharePoint team calendar. On the Calendar template, build a new list in order to construct a calendar. See Add a Calendar to a Page for instructions on adding an existing calendar to a different page.

SURVEY

An app that allows you to create questions that other users can respond to is called a survey. From basic lunch meeting settings to complex work process questionnaires, surveys can be used for a wide range of questions. There is no ribbon on the survey app. Rather, a Settings menu is used to control the settings.

Settings ▾

Add Questions
Add an additional question to this survey.

Survey Settings
Manage questions and settings for this survey.

77

MAKE A QUESTIONNAIRE

Similar to other programs, a survey is established, and you can then add your own questions to it. Depending on the kind of answer you wish to gather, you have a number of options to select from: Common response kinds include Rating Scale, Number, and Choice using radio buttons or a dropdown menu.

- Install the Survey app.
- Launch the most recent survey.
- Choose Add Questions after expanding the Settings accordion.
- Choose a question type and, if required, input options.
- Click Next Question to add more questions and repeat the process after adding the first one.
- Once all the questions have been added, click Finish.

EXAMINE BRANCHING LOGIC

You can use branching logic to determine which responses require a follow-up inquiry and which do not. You can use the Branching Logic option in each question to determine which question, based on the response, should come next. Once your questions have been entered, select the one that needs branching logic. For replies that shouldn't contain all

78

of the questions, you can choose the appropriate question to appear next under Jump To.

Possible Choices	Jump To
Every day	No Branching ⌄
Now and then	No Branching ⌄
Never	What should be the name of our next bicycle ⌄

ANSWER A QUESTIONNAIRE

A Respond link and survey information appear when a user opens the completed survey once it has been set up. To begin answering the questions, click the link.

VIEW SURVEY FINDINGS

You can view survey responses by selecting "Export to Spreadsheet" under Action or "show a graphical summary of the response" in the Survey dashboard after they have been

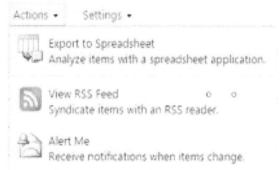

submitted. The survey's results are visible to all users who are able to reply.

All you need to do is refresh the Excel spreadsheet after exporting the data to add the new responses. Refer to Analyze SharePoint List Data in Excel to generate graphical representations of the survey responses from the Excel sheet.

ANNOUNCE THE RECORD

You can designate a file or list item as "record" when you wish to protect it. This indicates that you impose limitations on it that are independent of permissions. When declaring documents to be records, you usually wish to prevent them from being altered or removed. You can either create a workflow that declares a record or manually declare records on list items and files in document libraries. To manually declare things as records, you need to be an administrator or list contributor.

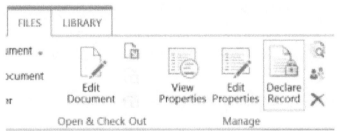

An icon on a file will have a lock when the file has been declared a record.

When you attempt to modify or remove a list item that has been declared as unmarked.

80

TURN ON THE ON-SITE RECORDS ADMINISTRATION

You must activate the In Place Records Management feature and provide the restriction settings, which are the same for the entire site collection, when you first set up manual records management in a site collection. First, go to Site Settings.

- In the Site Collection Administration group, select the "Site collection features" link.
- Turn on the In Place Records Management feature.

Following the activation of In Place Records Management, you need to specify which constraints have to be applied to files that are designated as records:

- First, go to Site Settings.
- In the Site Collection Administration group, select the "Record declaration settings" link.
- Customize the parameters to your liking.

PERMIT APP RECORD DECLARATION

You can choose whether manual records declaration should be available for all lists and libraries, as shown in the Record Declaration Settings image above. I advise you to leave the "Not available" option selected by default. I suggest

81

Jason Taylor

allowing record declaration for each app where you wish to use it, rather than providing a universal option to declare records. You will have greater control over how the functionality is used in this way:

- First, go to Library Settings.
- In the Permissions and Management group, select the "Record declaration settings" option.
- Using the site collection settings is the default record declaration setting.
- You must modify the site collection setting to "Always allow" for this library if it is set to "not available for all."

When files are added to the library, they can also be automatically declared as records using the Library declaration setting. Using this option eliminates the need to manually mark files as records. Alternatively, you can add files to this list that need to be declared records.

82

CHAPTER SEVEN

SHAREPOINT DESIGNER

Although it is free, SharePoint Designer is not part of the installation of any Office product. It must be installed via a Microsoft download or using Office 365 connections. Click the Settings gear on any Office 365 page to access the Office 365 settings, then select SharePoint Designer to install from within Office 365.

- Go to the Software area.
- To locate SharePoint Designer, open Tools & Add-ins.
- Select Install and Download. A new window with a download center is now displayed to you.
- Get the file and run it.

STEPS TO INSTALL SHAREPOINT DESIGNER

The steps to install SharePoint Designer are as follows:

- Use a search engine to find the Microsoft SharePoint Designer download page.
- Get the setup package.
- Launch the file that was downloaded.
- Agree to the terms of the license.
- Select the "Install Now" option.

- After the installation is complete, launch SharePoint Designer.

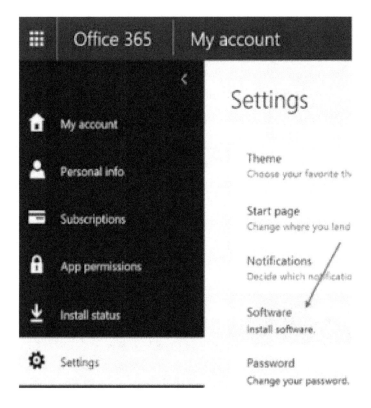

- You will receive a notification if you need to install the.NET Framework.
- To enable the.NET Framework, navigate to Control Panel > Programs & Features > Turn Windows features on and off.

84

- After then, you can use the link to install it.

- You will get the "Help Protect and Improve Microsoft Office" page when you first wish to open a site in SharePoint Designer.

- Don't use the suggested settings if you want to be able to access SharePoint Online sites in SharePoint Designer.

- Choose the "Don't make changes" option instead.

HOW TO USE SHAREPOINT DESIGNER TO OPEN THE SITE

Even if you wish to use an app, you should always open the site in SharePoint Designer. The app you wish to use can then be chosen.

- Select Open Site in SharePoint Designer.

- Type or paste the URL of the website you wish to access. Keep in mind that you should only enter the first portion of the URL that appears when you access the website.

- Select "Open."

- SharePoint Designer will now launch your SharePoint site.

- A summary page containing details about the chosen item is located to the right, while the site contents are

85

displayed to the left in a manner similar to a folder view.

HOW TO CREATE A LIST IN SHAREPOINT DESIGNER

You can use SharePoint Designer in place of making new lists on the web browser interface. It is faster and eliminates the need to click and load new pages.

- Launch SharePoint Designer and open the website.
- In the ribbon, click the SharePoint List button.
- Decide the list type to use.
- Click OK after giving the list a name and a description.

The SharePoint Designer summary page now displays the list options, allowing you to create your list faster than in SharePoint. In addition to adding, removing, and editing columns, views, and forms, you can choose settings. When the list is open in SharePoint Designer, you may use

the preview button above the ribbon or the keyboard shortcut F12 to see the list in the browser.

WORD ONLINE

Microsoft Word documents (.docx) open in Word Online by default when you are in a document library in SharePoint Online. Your document is automatically saved to the document library where it was generated when you use Word Online, which operates within the browser. Although Word Online lacks several features, it looks nearly identical to the desktop version of Word. On the other hand, several persons can edit a Word Online document simultaneously.

MULTIPLE USERS EDITING WORDS

You can choose to edit a Word document in the desktop version of Word or in Word Online when you open it in a library. You will be notified if you choose Word Online while someone else is editing the same document. Additionally, you can see where the other person is working in the document. You can carry on editing because the document will display all of the changes, regardless of who made them.

MODIFY THE WORD DOCUMENT TEMPLATE

A template can be made in two different methods. One is straightforward, and the other is a little trickier. Although I

87

will demonstrate the straightforward method here, I generally advise the more complex approach due to its greater advantages. You have the option to either edit the current template or provide a URL to a different template below. I'll go over how to update the current template here.

- Click the "Advanced settings" link after opening the Library options.
- Select the "(Edit Template)" link from the Advanced Settings page.
- A dialog box for an External Protocol Request will appear.
- Press the button to launch the application.
- You can make any necessary edits to the Word document that opens.
- Close and save the file. Now that you have your Word template, the template you have defined is not used when you click the "+ New" button to create a new document.
- You can only access your custom template by clicking on New Document under the ribbon's FILES tab.

88

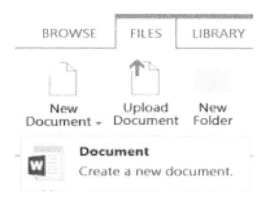

PERSONALIZE THE VIEW PAGE FOR DOCUMENTS

As can be seen above, the custom Word template is only utilized when a new document is created via the FILES tab button. You can alter the document view page to include a link to the template if you would like an alternate method of accessing it.

For this solution to function, the template needs to be in a file share. Following this, you can include a web section on the document view page that contains a link to the template that should be used, or to a number of templates.

- Select "Edit page" from the "Settings" menu in the upper right corner of the page.
- Select the "Add a Web Part" link.

89

- Choose the "Content Editor" online section under the "Media and Content" category.
- Press the "Add" button.
- Click "Edit Web Part" after expanding the web part tool pin accordion.
- Expand "Appearance" under "Test Link" and scroll down to "Chrome Type" to eliminate the web component caption. After choosing "None," click "Apply."
- Create a display text and use Link to a File Server to link it to a file server or to a particular template.
- Select "Stop Editing" from the ribbon's "PAGE" tab.

A NOTE

In the Quick Launch, there is a Notebook link for every SharePoint team site. It launches OneNote, Microsoft's note-taking application included in the Office suite, in its online edition.

Having OneNote Online in SharePoint makes it simple to share with other team members, and it functions nicely in the browser. The Site Assets library on each team site contains the default OneNote notebook as well as every other notebook you make.

90

You can add text, graphics, and links using a variety of options when you launch OneNote Online by clicking on the Notebook link in the Quick Launch.

When you create a new file in a document library with the default content type, you are presented with a number of default file types, including the notebook file type (see Create a file in a library). By selecting the Notebooks icon located in the upper left corner of OneNote Online, you may access all of the team site's notebooks.

You can Edit Links and take the Quick Launch link down if you don't want users to have access to OneNote. Existing

notebooks in the Site Assets library can also be removed. To change OneNote's default settings when creating a new document in a library, you must modify the library's content type.

FOLDERS IN LIBRARY

The most often used but least advised method of characterization in SharePoint is the old and tested folder. Nevertheless, there are certain advantages, particularly when utilizing OneDrive for Business or the "Open with Windows Explorer" option; see Import Files and Folders from Windows Explorer.

The primary justification for folders is that, in contrast to file servers, users will feel more at home and that there will be no need to alter the way data is kept. You will soon discover, though, that folders have a number of significant disadvantages. SharePoint has numerous major folder-related annoyances and isn't really designed to handle folders well. You can hide the folder option if you don't want users to be able to create new library folders, as explained below.

92

MAKE A NEW FOLDER

You can either click on New and choose New folder, or you can click the New Folder option under the FILES tab in the ribbon to create a folder in a SharePoint library.

Click on Create after giving the folder a name that indicates the type of files it contains.

TRANSFER FILES BETWEEN FOLDERS

You can drag and drop documents into a folder by clicking on the file type icon to the left of the file name. Click the file type icon to the left of the file name, then drag

93

and drop the file onto the Quick Launch document library link to remove it from a folder.

THE OPTION TO HIDE THE FOLDER

By default, you might also create a folder when you click on +new in SharePoint libraries. In general, I advise against using library folders. You can hide the option to prevent users from creating folders in Library Settings >Advanced Settings if you agree.

DISTRIBUTE A FILE OR DIRECTORY

Using the standard Permissions settings, library files and folders can be shared with individuals outside the organization. To share a file or folder, click the ellipsis next to it and choose SHARE. You may now begin entering the name of the individual or people who ought to have access. After that, you will have options to choose from. "Can edit" is the default permission when sharing. Perhaps you should replace that to "Can view." An email invitation is issued by default, but if you prefer to notify others about the sharing, you can uncheck that item. If you choose the "Everyone" option, no emails will be sent. You can also obtain the shared file or folder link in this box.

94

CHAPTER EIGHT

BUSINESS ONEDRIVE

SharePoint users can add and edit libraries as folders on their PCs or other smart devices using the online service OneDrive for Business. Both a manual synchronization and an automatic synchronization occur when the user is logged into SharePoint. Here, I'll walk you through setting up a synchronization between a folder on your computer and a SharePoint library.

HOW TO BEGIN SYNC BETWEEN THE PC FOLDER AND THE SHAREPOINT LIBRARY

OneDrive for Business will monitor changes and synchronize this library and folder automatically after you have set up the synchronization between the library and your PC, but you will need to do it manually the first time. If you need to make a manual sync, you can also follow the procedures below at any time. Normally, you shouldn't need to use the download URL found in the initial "Sync now" box because OneDrive for Business is part of the Office 365 subscription.

- Click the Sync button above the files or under the ribbon LIBRARY tab after opening the document

95

library containing the files you wish to synchronize to your computer.

- In the first dialog, select Sync now. In the second window, select Sync now once more.

- OneDrive for Business generates a new "SharePoint" folder on your computer if this is your first time synchronizing a SharePoint library. The path to that folder is displayed in the second "Sync now" box.

- Next, a new folder is created by OneDrive for Business inside the SharePoint folder. It receives both the library's name and the name of the SharePoint site.

- The new folder displays every file in the SharePoint library. They are synced, as shown by their green flag.

- File transfers between the new SharePoint folder and your other folders will run smoothly if you add it to your Favorites/Quick Access list.

MYSITE

MySite is a personal SharePoint site collection that uses OneDrive for Business. Unless the user chooses to share the files, they remain private. Each user of the Office 365 Enterprise subscription tiers has unlimited capacity in the MySite collection for OneDrive for Business.

96

I advise you to add new libraries to the MySite site collection because the default MySite library, Files, is lacking in functionality. They will provide you with more alternatives than the Files library because they will contain all the capabilities of the SharePoint library.

Actually, each user can access the full range of SharePoint capability by adding more apps and subsites to a collection of MySite sites. Since every user manages their own collection of sites, the options are essentially limitless. I'll go over how SharePoint users can benefit from MySite in this part.

HOW TO GET TO MYSITE

Your personal MySite site collection will open when you click on the OneDrive icon in the Office 365 App Launcher.

- Click on Create after giving the folder a name that indicates the type of files it contains.

97

HOW TO TRANSFER FILES BETWEEN FOLDERS

- You can drag and drop documents into a folder by clicking on the file type icon to the left of the file name.

- Click the file type icon to the left of the file name, then drag and drop the file onto the Quick Launch document library link to remove it from a folder.

- Refer to Import Files and Folders from Windows Explorer to learn how to create folders, move documents, and open the document library in Windows Explorer while using Internet Explorer.

THE OPTION TO HIDE THE FOLDER

By default, you might also create a folder when you click on +new in SharePoint libraries. In general, I advise against using library folders. You can hide the option to prevent users from creating folders in Library Settings >Advanced Settings if you agree.

DISTRIBUTE A FILE OR DIRECTORY

Using the standard Permissions settings, library files and folders can be shared with individuals outside the organization. To share a file or folder, click the ellipsis next to it and choose SHARE. You may now begin entering the name of the individual or people who ought to have access.

98

After that, you will have options to choose from. "Can edit" is the default permission when sharing. Perhaps you should replace that to "Can view." An email invitation is issued by default, but if you prefer to notify others about the sharing, you can uncheck that item. If you choose the "Everyone" option, no emails will be sent. You can also obtain the shared file or folder link in this box.

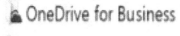

EDIT PAGES

Customization of SharePoint Wiki Pages is possible. In the page's content sections, you can easily add text, links, images, videos, and more. Additionally, you can alter and add other types of Web Parts. Although not as much, Web Part Pages can also be modified.

USE EDIT MODE TO OPEN A PAGE

A page must be opened in edit mode before you may make changes to it. If the page is a wiki page as opposed to a web component page, this is handled differently. Only the wiki page has an EDIT link, therefore you can tell which page it is by looking in the upper right corner.

LAUNCH EDIT MODE ON THE WIKI PAGE

A wiki page can be opened in edit mode in three different ways:

- In the upper right corner of the page, click the EDIT link.
- On the ribbon PAGE tab, select the Edit button.
- In the Office 365 panel, click the settings gear and choose Edit page.

Edit mode will be used when the page opens. A SAVE button under the PAGE tab and a SAVE link in the upper right corner will now take the place of the Edit button and link. To add content, move the mouse pointer to the desired location.

LAUNCH EDIT MODE ON THE WEB PART PAGE

Click the settings gear in the Office 365 panel and choose Edit page to access a web part page in edit mode. This option is identical to the third one for the wiki pages mentioned above. Edit mode will be used when the page opens. Under the ribbon's PAGE tab, there will now be a Stop Editing button. Clicking on this button will save the page automatically.

Add or edit web components to change the page.

100

EDIT THE PAGE ON THE WIKI

Although wiki pages are written in HTML, Microsoft has made it simple to edit them and add content using a variety

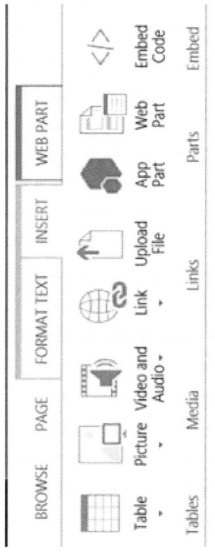

101

of tools on the SharePoint ribbon. Reversing modifications is also simple. You should be aware that there are limitations on using CSS and JavaScript if you wish to use HTML code. I'll only demonstrate how to access the HTML code here; I'll concentrate on using the SharePoint tools for no-code customization. You can add and modify web elements to the wiki page in addition to directly altering the page itself.

Take a look at the page

As you edit the page, you should review it. This prevents other people from editing the same page simultaneously. To check out, click the Check Out button located under the ribbon's PAGE tab. When you are done editing, you can use the Check In button that has now taken the position of the Check Out button. There will be a warning on the page as well.

⚠ **Status:** Checked out and editable.

The page will stay checked out if you save it without checking out. In order to allow other users to modify the page and view the edited version, you must check the box. The page will automatically save if you check it in without saving first.

102

REQUIRED CHECK-OUT

You can configure the Site Pages library to always demand check-out of pages that enter edit mode if you're worried about editing conflicts. This is applied to every page in the Site Pages collection and is done under the Versioning Settings.

- First, access the Site Contents, followed by the Site Pages.
- After selecting the ellipsis, click the SETTINGS link. 3. Navigate to the General Settings group and select the Versioning settings.
- In the "Require documents to be checked out before they can be edited" field, select "Yes." (Remember, pages are also papers.)

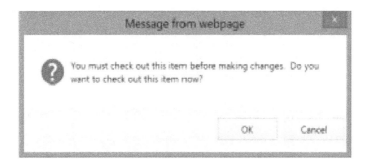

103

- After this configuration is completed, a warning notice appears when a user tries to edit a page, and they must click OK to view the page.

Enter and Format Text Just as in Word and other Office programs, you may enter and format text in a wiki page. To begin writing, move the mouse pointer to the desired location. Numerous text formatting choices are available under the ribbon's FORMAT TEXT tab. Using the Undo button or the Ctrl key + z key, you can quickly undo changes. Press Ctrl + y to do it again.

I advise you to use styles rather than the Font ribbon group's controls. Under the FORMAT TEXT tab, farther to the right, is the Styles ribbon group. A Styles library that is shared by a site and all of its subsites contains the styles. Editing the styles to your liking takes some effort, but once you have them, you may use them on other pages as well. Your SharePoint site will seem consistent thanks to the styles, and you can easily alter them if you want to. All pages that utilize that style will then have the modification implemented.

INCORPORATE A FILE

Using the embed code, Word, PDF, and PowerPoint files can be included on SharePoint wiki pages. Click on the ellipsis to the right of the file, then on the menu to locate the embed code.

105

- Select the Embed Information option from the menu beneath the image. Make a copy of the embed code.
- Click the Embed Code button after selecting the INSERT tab on the page.
- Paste the embed code for the picture into the form, making any necessary modifications.
- Press the Insert button.

INCLUDE A TABLE

Although adding a table to a SharePoint wiki page is not as simple or feature-rich as it is in Word, it is still feasible and manageable.

- Select the Table button from the INSERT tab.
- To launch a dialog, choose Insert Table; alternatively, utilize the grid beneath the button.
- Either drag the mouse over the desired number of columns and rows in the grid, or enter the number of columns and rows you want the table to have in the Insert Table dialog.
- The table will be added to the page when you click OK in the dialog box OR release the mouse.

TABLE LAYOUT and DESIGN are the two new table tool tabs that appear when you move the mouse pointer inside the table. The table can be edited here.

106

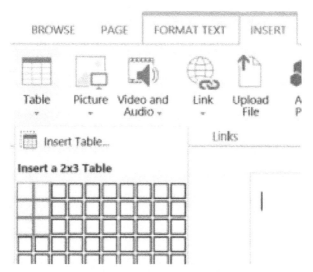

You can copy and paste the table onto the SharePoint page if you would rather design it in Word or another Office program.

CHAPTER NINE

MODIFY THE SOURCE

The Edit Source button is located beneath the FORMAT TEXT tab, much to the right in the ribbon. This control allows you to edit or paste code from another editor by opening the web portion in HTML. Keep in mind that just the body code is shown, and that JavaScript and CSS have some restrictions. Additionally, see Add Custom JavaScript to a Page and Add Custom CSS to a Page.

PRESERVE

To preserve your edits, you must save the page after you're done.

- Press on the SAVE button in the page's upper right corner. Under the PAGE and FORMAT TEXT tabs on the ribbon, you may also select the Save button.
- There are more options on the Save button. To remove your edits, use the Stop Editing option.

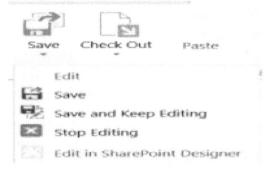

108

BRING BACK PREVIOUS VERSIONS

The Undo button cannot be used once the page has been saved. You can, however, restore a previous version of the page if necessary because versioning is enabled on pages by default. The Page History button is located under the PAGE tab on the ribbon. After selecting the version, you wish to restore, click Restore this version. Additionally, you can use the Site Content to restore previous versions. On the page you have been modifying, click the ellipsis after selecting the Site Pages icon. Locate Version History, pick the desired version, and then choose Restore from the drop-down menu.

INTRODUCTION TO WEB PARTS

A SharePoint web part is a component that can be added to a SharePoint page and is typically used to fill in content. For various types of content, there are distinct web sections. Although web parts are the foundation of all SharePoint pages, only Wiki Pages and Web Part Pages allow you to modify the web parts. I advise you to look over the web sections. Because you can always go back and restore earlier versions if you make a mistake, it's a safe place to work.

APP COMPONENTS

From the standpoint of the user, web parts and app parts are comparable, and some components are included under both

109

categories. I therefore skip over the distinctions here. App parts can be used similarly to web parts.

HOW TO GET STARTED

The "Get started with your site" web section is automatically included when you establish a team website. "Get started with your site" offers five links that are referred to as Promoted Links and are shown as tiles. Because Microsoft has included a "REMOVE THIS" link to remove the "Get Started with your site" web element, it is the only part of the page that may be deleted without first launching the page in edit mode. You must add the Get Started web component again, just like you would other web parts; see Add a Web component to a Wiki Page below for instructions.

INCLUDE A WEB SECTION

Depending on whether the page is a wiki page or a web part page, there are various methods for adding web parts.

To add a web element to a wiki page, follow these general steps:

- Launch Edit Mode on the Wiki Page.
- Move the mouse pointer to the desired location for the web portion.
- Click the Web Part button after selecting the INSERT tab.

110

- Decide on a group.

- Click the Add button after selecting a web section.

- Add or modify the web portion as you see fit.

- Click the Save button or link to save the modifications. The modifications will be saved, and Edit will once more take the place of Save.

ADD A WEB PART TO A WEB PART PAGE

Adding a web part to a web part page is best done by using a link to add the web part to the top of the page; this way, the page is published rather than saved. The steps are the same else.

- Launch Edit Mode on the Web Part Page.

- On top of the page, click the Add a Web Part option.

- Decide on a group.

- Click the Add button after selecting a web section.

(If you don't want the new web element to be on top, drag and drop it or drag other web parts above it.)

- Add or modify the web portion as you see fit.

- Click the Save button or link to save the modifications.

- To allow other users to access the page, publish it. Additionally, you can submit it for approval.

111

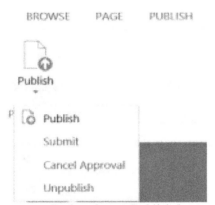

- Rather than a Publish button, web component pages occasionally include a Stop Editing button.

MODIFY THE WEB SECTION

- Click the arrow in the web part's upper right corner and choose Edit Web Part to change the web part's properties. Additionally, you can decrease and

112

remove the online portion here, and you can export certain web sections to your computer.

- To use the Edit Web Part command, click the Web Part Properties button after selecting the WEB PART tab.

The web part's name appears in the top banner of the Edit Web Part panel, which is displayed to the right of the web component. Although the appearance of these panels varies depending on the site section, they consistently offer a number of options. The panel for a Documents web component can be seen in the picture below.

GIVE A PAGE A CALENDAR

Instead of keeping your team calendar in a separate list, you should definitely display it on a page, perhaps the team site's home page.

- Go to Edit Mode and open a page.
- Include a Web Part, such as your recently developed calendar application. It is also located under App Part.
- Make any necessary changes to the Web Part Design and save the page.

113

THE WEB SECTION OF THE CONTENT EDITOR

The only way to add text, photos, and other elements to a web page in SharePoint and prior was through the Content Editor web section. This is still how it operates, so you will have all the options you have in Wiki Pages when you add the Content Editor web component to Web component Pages and edit them.

When you insert and focus the Content Editor web element, a ribbon with numerous options will appear. As a result, adding the Content Editor web part to a web part page to provide it the same functionality as a wiki page is the most popular use case for it.

However, there are also justifications for using the Content Editor web section in wiki sites. For instance, you can use the Content Editor to add JavaScript and CSS to a page, which is not possible on a wiki page; see Add Custom JavaScript to a Page and Add Custom CSS to a Page. The Media and Content category include the Content Editor web section. To prevent the Content Editor caption from appearing on the web component, edit the web part and set the Chrome Type to None.

The entire company can use enterprise keywords. They are centrally controlled in the Term Store and synchronized

114

across all of the tenant's lists and libraries. This implies that if a user adds a keyword to one library, it will appear as a suggestion when they begin writing a similar word in that library or another.

Include a column for enterprise keywords. Open the List Settings and select Enterprise Metadata and Keywords Settings under Permissions and Management to add an Enterprise Keywords column to a SharePoint list or library. You can check the Enterprise Keywords box here.

Upon completion, the library gains an Enterprise Keywords

Permissions and Management

- Delete this list
- Save list as template
- Permissions for this list
- Workflow Settings
- Generate file plan report
- Enterprise Metadata and Keywords Settings
- Information management policy settings

column of the Managed Metadata type. However, it is only visible when you open a document's properties. To make it visible in the library or list views, I advise you to modify the view.

115

USE ENTERPRISE KEYWORDS WHEN TAGGING

Use enterprise keywords such as these to tag documents and list items: In the Enterprise Keywords field, type the keyword for a list item after opening it. Enter the term in the Enterprise Keywords area of the Edit File Properties dialog box for a document. You can also open the list or library in Quick Edit mode and type the keyword in the Enterprise Keywords field after adding the Enterprise Keywords column to the view. Once you begin writing, you will always have options to choose from.

THE TERM STORE

Any user with write rights on a list or library can add keywords to the Enterprise Keywords folksonomy, which makes them accessible to all tenants. The idea of tagging is widely recognized from social media, and typically, SharePoint allows users to freely contribute keywords, or tags. The SharePoint Admin Center is where you go if you still need to change the keywords, like deleting improperly spelled or inappropriate terms. To do this, you must have access to SharePoint or an Office 365 tenant's global administrative role.

- Select the "term store" link located on the left side of the SharePoint Admin Center.
- The first time, add yourself as the Term Store Administrator.
- Move or remove keywords by opening the Keywords accordion.

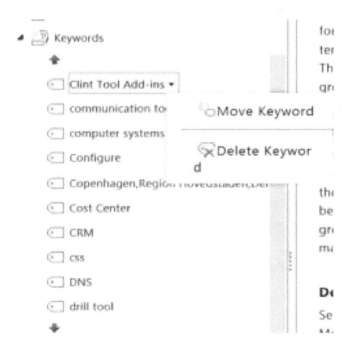

The Enterprise Keywords column should be removed. You just check a box in the library settings to add the Enterprise Keywords column; however, you cannot uncheck

117

the same box to delete the column. The column will remain visible when you access an item's properties, even though you can obviously delete it from any view. You must follow the same steps as for other columns in order to remove the Enterprise Keywords column from a SharePoint application; see Delete a Column. The Enterprise Keywords are still available in the Term Store and can be utilized in other apps even after the column has been removed. They must be deleted from the Term Store if you wish to get rid of them completely.

OVERSIDE METADATA

SharePoint automatically adds the keywords you enter in that column to the Term Store when you utilize Enterprise Keywords. Additionally, you have the ability to create various groups of terms and administer the Term Store yourself. In this instance, the keywords' column type can be anything, but it needs to be the same type as the Enterprise Keywords column, which is Managed Metadata.

UPDATE THE TERM STORE WITH KEYWORDS

Although you can obviously add keywords to existing term sets and term sets to existing groups in the same manner as explained below, this is how to add a new term store group and term set.

118

- Right-click on Taxonomy, the top level in the Term Store, and choose New Group.
- Give the new group a name.
- You can either click on Import Term Set to import data from a CSV file or right-click on the new group to add a New Term Set.
- To add more Term Sets, hit Enter.
- To add keywords, right-click on each term set.
- Select "Save."

ATTACH THE TERM STORE TO A COLUMN

To utilize the keywords kept in the Term Store and link a column to it, create a column, select the Managed Metadata column type radio button, and give it any name you want.

You may then link the column to one of your term sets in the Create Column dialog. Enter a term, and all term sets that contain that phrase will be displayed. Choose the term set's highest level to utilize. Now, every keyword you add to this column will be saved in the term set you linked it to, and users can suggest any keyword in the term set. Of course, you can also modify the term set to which a Managed Metadata column is attached or open an existing Managed Metadata column from the library settings to connect it to a term set.

119

CHAPTER TEN

LIBRARY FILES' CATEGORIES

All of your files can be placed directly into a large document library with numerous folders inside of folders when sharing documents in SharePoint. Along with the extra features of version history, full text search, workflows, views, and alarms, most things will function as they would on a file server. However, there are better options! All of the above-mentioned classification techniques are effective for all apps, including libraries; however, I will now discuss a few more techniques that are unique to libraries.

SEVERAL LIBRARIES

It soon becomes clear which files belong in your document library and which don't once you begin using Views and Columns. Continuing with the hotel example I began above, it would be absurd to fill out the "Mode of transportation" box for a hotel and the "Swimming Pool" option for an expedition.

It makes reasonable to construct a separate document library for each of those information types rather than attempting to fit both hotels and excursions into one document library. In general, it's a good idea to use various libraries for different types of files. Using many libraries rather than just one

120

library with folders improves the performance of these four features:

- Search
- Permissions
- Navigation, and
- Scaling.

If you place all of your documents in one library, you will eventually need to shift them to other libraries because a SharePoint document library shouldn't have more than 5000 items.

RATE DOCUMENTS

In SharePoint document libraries, users can rate files either by stars or by likes. Rating offers a number of advantages: The column can be filtered by rating. Views might be generated according to the rating. The search results are displayed in order of rating. The most popular and highly rated songs are automatically shown first.

TURN ON RATING

Navigate to the Library Settings and select the Rating settings link under General Settings to enable rating in a library.

121

At this point, you can permit rating and choose whether to utilize stars or likes. The default view will display a newly created rating column. Of course, you may add it to any other view as well; see Modify a View.

Settings › Rating Settings

Rating settings

Specify whether or not items in this list can be rated.

When you enable ratings, two fields are added to the content types available for this list and a rating control is added to the default view of the list or library. You can

Allow items in this list to be rated?

○ Yes
● No

Which voting/rating experience you would like to enable for this list?

○ Likes
○ Star Ratings

122

FILE RATES

can rate each file by clicking on one of the five blank stars in the star rating column. You should click on the third star if you wish to rate a file with three stars because doing so will fill all the stars to the left. When you click on the Like link in the like rating, a smiley face appears at the file. By selecting "Unlike," the linking can be eliminated. SharePoint also displays the number of users who have rated the file in both situations.

LINKS

Everything on the internet is built on links. A link, officially known as a hyperlink, is a reference to a particular document, image, sound, section, or web page. Another name for it is a shortcut or URL. In SharePoint, a link is identified when you hover over text or an image and the mouse pointer change into a hand. The link will frequently be underlined and highlighted when you hover over the text.

ADD WIKI PAGE LINKS

There are two ways to add links to Wiki Pages: "From SharePoint" and "From Address." The ribbon's INSERT tab contains both. The page must first be opened in edit mode.

123

Next, select the text or image you wish to link to, or move the mouse pointer to the desired location.

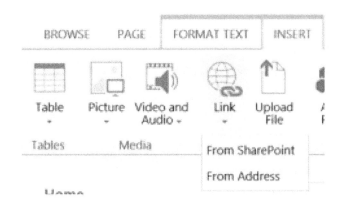

USING SHAREPOINT

When adding a link to a page within the same site collection, use the "From SharePoint" link option. You can choose the location to link to on a new page that appears when you choose "From SharePoint."

FROM THE ADDRESS

When adding a link to a page that is not part of your SharePoint Online or even the site collection, use the "From Address" link option. When you choose "From Address', a window allowing you to enter a URL will appear.

124

It will be filled out under Text to display if you have selected a text. If not, you can enter text that will be displayed as an anchor. Before clicking OK, you can also try the link.

Right-click on a link and choose Copy Shortcut to make a copy. After that, you can paste it anywhere you want to add it, including in the "From Address" dialog.

OPTIONS FOR LINKS

The LINK tab will open when the mouse pointer is placed next to the new link. You can add a description here, and when users hover their mouse over the link, a pop-up window will appear. The webpage you are linking to can also have a bookmark added to it, which you can enter under the LINK tab. At that bookmark, the page will then open. If you have linked to an Office file and would like an icon to indicate the file type, check the Display icon box. Otherwise, all you will see is a blank white icon. You can also remove a link and open the link location under the LINK tab, as well as set the link location to open in a new tab.

IN LISTS, ADD LINKS

The first step in adding a link to a list is to create a column in the list that is either an image or a hyperlink. Choose to

 Hyperlink or Picture

125

format the URL as a hyperlink and give the column a name. A link can be added to the new column in one of two ways: Copy or enter the URL in the new column while in Quick Edit mode. You will receive the link without any display text as a result. To add the URL, open the list item in Standard mode. You can now type display text.

Type the Web address: (Click here to test)

http://

Type the description:

If the Enhanced Rich text radio button is selected, you can also add links in columns of the Multiple lines of text type. You will have the same Link Options in the ribbon when you add links to a page as when you open an item and type in a multiple-line text field.

ADD NEWSFEED LINKS

Links can be added to a Newsfeed by typing or pasting the URL. You will be able to type or paste a different display text than the link if you press Enter after entering the URL. Before clicking Post to publish the entire Newsfeed entry, click the check icon to save the display text.

126

LINK AN IMAGE

You can link an image to a wiki page in the same way that you link text.

- Go to Edit Mode and open a page.
- Pick the picture from the page.
- Click the Link button after selecting the INSERT tab.
- When choosing where to point the image link, pick one of the two options.
- Click OK after choosing the location or entering the address, depending on the option.
- Pick the picture. The ribbon will display two more tabs: LINK and IMAGE.
- Edit the link by selecting the LINK or IMAGE tab.

A FILE SERVER LINK

You can provide a link on the page if you want to quickly access a file from a SharePoint page without uploading it to SharePoint. Any file server address (UNC) can be linked to.

- To link the network folder to a SharePoint page, copy its link.
- Click the Link button on the ribbon's INSERT tab after opening a page in Edit Mode.
- Pick the "From Address" choice.

127

- Enter the address using the File: //[folder link] format.
- Click OK after writing a text display.
- Select the link to open in a new page and click on it to display the LINK tab.
- Save the page.

The page will now display the folder link. A warning will appear when you click on the link. The associated network folder will open when you click "Allow." Additionally, you can link to a particular file server document.

- Choose Create shortcut from the menu when you right-click on the document file on the file server.
- Choose Properties with a right-click on the shortcut.
- In the Target field, copy the path. The complete link, including File: //, will be displayed to you.
- As previously mentioned, add the link to the SharePoint page.

It is also possible to obtain the correct link from within an Office document.

- Launch the document, then select Editing.

128

- Click on the file location in the Info menu under the FILE tab, then choose Copy link to clipboard. You will also receive the complete link, including File: //, as a result.

LINKING TO WIKI

You can accomplish tasks that are challenging to handle in other ways by adding wiki links to wiki pages. For instance, you can use wiki links to point to an uncreated page. Open the page in Edit mode (see Open a Page in Edit Mode). Wiki connections are only functional within a single site. This implies that although you can connect to pages, lists, libraries, and even a specific view or item, you are unable to utilize a wiki link to refer to anything outside of SharePoint or on another site or site collection. Links must begin and end with double square brackets, [[...]], and the wiki link syntax must be entered. A list of all the pages, lists, and views on a SharePoint wiki page will appear when you write the first two brackets in edit mode. The closing brackets will be added automatically when you select one of the alternatives.

129

If you wish to connect to a page that doesn't exist, for instance, you can enter the syntax in rather than choosing. The closing brackets must then be manually added as well.

HOW TO CREATE A PAGE AND LINK TO A WIKI

Wiki links allow you to make the link first, followed by the page you're linking to:

- Write the new page's name in double square brackets, like this: [[Sales]].
- To indicate that the page does not yet exist, a dotted underline will appear around the link after you save the page.
- You will be prompted to create the page after clicking on the link.
- To customize the new page, click Create. This will open the page in edit mode.
- The link will take you to the page you just generated and will no longer be underlined when you return to the page where you created it.

PROMOTED LINKS

Links in the form of moving tiles appear on the start page of a SharePoint Online team site when you initially create it. You may make these links yourself and add them to any SharePoint page. They are known as promoted links.

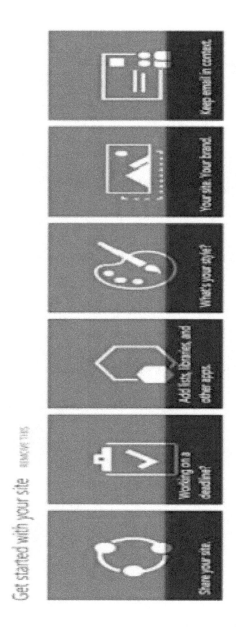

131

MAKE LINKS THAT ARE PROMOTED

Make use of the command Create a Promoted Links app by adding an app.

- Go to the All Promoted Links screen after launching the Promoted Links app.
- Select "+ new item." You can add links to the background picture and link location, a description, and the tile's order in the dialog that appears.
- You can also choose whether the link location opens in a dialog box, a new tab, or the same page. After completing the form, click Save.
- For every tile, repeat step 2.
- Take the application out of Quick Launch.

IMAGES OF PROMOTED LINKS

Although it is not required, you are free to use any image in the promoted links if you so like. If you choose a larger image, it will be compressed because the size will be 150x150 pixels. A smaller image will result in poor quality, so avoid utilizing it. Only code can be used to alter the size of promoted links.

132

Include the App for Promoted Links on a Page
The Promoted Links application can be added to any
SharePoint page after it has been established.

- Go to Edit Mode on the page.
- Click the App Part button under the INSERT tab after
  positioning the mouse pointer where you want the
  application to appear.
- Pick the recently developed Promoted Links
  application.
- Before saving, make any desired adjustments to the
  app portion.

CONNECT AND EXPORT SHAREPOINT DATA

You can access the Connect & Export ribbon group under
the LIST/LIBRARY/CALENDAR tab. These platforms
allow you to open SharePoint lists and utilize features that
facilitate working with the data.

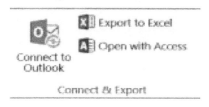

There is an additional button for synchronization with
Project in SharePoint lists that are based on the Tasks

133

template: see Sync SharePoint Tasks list with Project. I'll demonstrate a number of methods in this chapter for integrating and synchronizing SharePoint with Outlook, Excel, Project, and Access. In addition to comparing Excel and SharePoint, I will describe how the results of connections to Excel differ from those to Outlook, Project, and Access. Additionally, I'll provide some examples of how Access and SharePoint can work together. Displaying Excel content as a web part on a SharePoint page is an additional method of connecting. Similar steps can be taken with Visio drawings as well.

LINK THE OUTLOOK AND SHAREPOINT

Numerous semi-hidden features in the Calendar, Tasks, and Contacts list types enable synchronization with Outlook. Additionally, you can sync your personal Outlook with SharePoint libraries. To establish the connection, use the "Connect to Outlook" button located under the LIST/LIBRARY/CALENDAR tab.

Connect to
Outlook

134

THE VIEW OF OUTLOOK FOLDERS

In the Outlook Folders view, lists and libraries that are synchronized with Outlook are shown under the name SharePoint Lists.

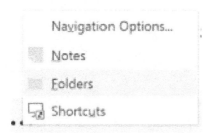

Click the ellipses (…) in the lower left corner of any Outlook view to bring up the Folders view. (The Outlook Contacts/Calendar view similarly shows the lists of contacts and calendars.)

INTEGRATE OUTLOOK WITH A SHAREPOINT LIBRARY

When you link a SharePoint library to Outlook, you can work offline with the library files. Keep in mind that only

135

the files themselves are synced, not the metadata. In the Outlook Folders view, the library files are categorized under a different heading. In order to work with a file in Outlook, you must first select the Edit Offline button. The files will then be synchronized to SharePoint the next time you are logged into SharePoint Online, allowing you to edit and save them as normal. You can utilize other Outlook settings, such as send and receive settings, on the SharePoint-synchronized folder since you have the files in Outlook.

INTEGRATE OUTLOOK WITH A SHAREPOINT CALENDAR

Connecting the SharePoint team calendar to your own Outlook is frequently helpful because Outlook offers more calendar functionality than SharePoint. If you do that, Outlook will display the SharePoint calendar as a different calendar. You will see the events on the team calendar when you refresh your SharePoint page because any new events you create using Outlook will be synchronized to SharePoint.

The "Calendar" calendar in the Outlook calendar view in the image below is your personal calendar, which is typically kept in your Exchange mailbox. The "HR-HR Events" calendar is a SharePoint calendar. The site's name (HR) and

136

the calendar list's name (HR Events) are the two components of the name.

Both calendars will be shown side by side when the boxes are checked, and you may copy and paste events or drag and drop them from one calendar to the other. If you wish to view a single calendar, uncheck one of the boxes. Just like with your personal calendar, you can use colors in Outlook to group events in the SharePoint calendar. However, at least as of the publication of this book, SharePoint does not display these colors.

INTEGRATE OUTLOOK WITH A SHAREPOINT CONTACTS LIST

A SharePoint contacts list will appear in Outlook under Other Contacts when you link it to your personal account. When you create new contacts in that Outlook folder, they will be synchronized to SharePoint and appear in the contacts list when you reload the SharePoint website. "HR- Consultants" is the SharePoint contacts list in the HR site, as seen in the image below from the Outlook contacts' view.

137

◢ My Contacts

Contacts

◢ Other Contacts

HR - Consultants

Contacts between My Contacts and Other Contacts can be copied and pasted or dropped. In this instance, the "Contacts" are kept in the Exchange mailbox, and the "HR-Consultants" are kept in SharePoint.

INTEGRATE OUTLOOK WITH A SHAREPOINT TASKS LIST

You can work with the tasks while offline when you connect a SharePoint Tasks list to Outlook. The SharePoint list is added to the Outlook Tasks as a distinct tasks folder. The tasks will be synchronized as soon as you re-establish your connection to SharePoint. You can drag and drop or copy and paste between the Exchange and SharePoint tasks, just like you can with contacts and calendars. The SharePoint tasks list on the IT site is represented by the "IT-IT-tasks" in the figure below, which is taken from the Outlook tasks view.

138

DELETE AN OUTLOOK SYNCHRONIZED LIST

It is quite simple to delete the synchronized SharePoint list from Outlook if you no longer have an Office 365 license or for any other reason don't want it there:

- Launch the Outlook Folders dialog box.
- Navigate to the SharePoint lists by scrolling down.
- To delete a list, right-click on it and choose Delete Folder.
- In the confirmation dialog, select Yes.

HOW TO ADD A CALENDAR FROM OUTLOOK TO SHAREPOINT

The Connect to Outlook functionality allows you to import calendar data from an Outlook calendar to a new SharePoint calendar.

- Add an application to SharePoint; in this example, a calendar app.
- Link the updated calendar to Outlook by following the instructions in Connect SharePoint to Outlook.
- In Outlook, switch the original Outlook calendar's view to List view.
- Make a copy of the whole Outlook calendar.
- Launch the SharePoint calendar and select List as the view.

139

- In the SharePoint calendar, paste every item you copied from the original Outlook calendar.

This technique can even be used to import a calendar ICS file into SharePoint from another location, such a website.

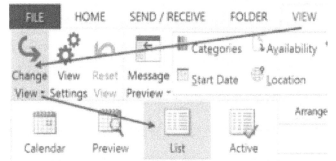

As an intermediary step, use Outlook to import the external calendar first, and then, as previously mentioned, copy the items to the synchronized SharePoint calendar in Outlook.

140

CHAPTER ELEVEN

LINK EXCEL AND SHAREPOINT

Excel and SharePoint lists have many features, but they can differ significantly. Despite not being designed with data sharing in mind, Microsoft Excel is frequently used in this manner. Conversely, SharePoint provides benefits that make it better suited for data sharing than Excel because it was created with collaboration in mind from the start: editing. When someone is modifying a SharePoint list, it does not lock. On a file server, an Excel file is locked to prevent unauthorized access until the editing process is complete and the updated file has been saved.

VERSIONING: Every row in a list can have previous versions shown and restored via SharePoint. Since Excel lacks a versioning tool, you must give multiple versions of a file alternative names. Even then, you will still need to manually identify the differences between the two files. Warnings.

The Alert feature in SharePoint lists allows you to receive an automated email whenever a list item is modified. When this alert should be sent can be set in a number of ways. Additionally, you can use SharePoint Workflows to build

141

more sophisticated notifications. This is not possible in Excel without a lot of coding.

AUTONOMY: Because each item in a SharePoint list is independent of the others, you can define independent row permissions and modify and lock each row (=item). Additionally, you should be aware of the following issues with SharePoint: mobility. Transferring a SharePoint list is more difficult than an Excel file. (This might be viewed as advantageous as well! The ease with which an Excel file can be shared is not always a benefit.

RELOCATION EXPENSES AND RETRAINING: The process of transferring data from Excel to SharePoint will take some time. Allowing individuals to continue working as they have always done is always simpler! the list limit of 5000 entries. There is now a 5000 item limit on lists in a view in SharePoint Online. Therefore, if the data yields more than 5000 list items, you need divide it up. (An additional choice is to share Excel files in SharePoint by uploading them to a library.)

According to the conclusion, SharePoint offers many more sharing options, thus anything that needs to be shared should be stored there. Excel, on the other hand, has great capabilities for analysis, computation, and visualization. The

142

good news is that you can also utilize these Excel functionalities on the data in your SharePoint lists!

HOW TO EXPORT A LIST FROM SHAREPOINT TO EXCEL

You may benefit from Excel's superior analytical, computation, and visualization capabilities by exporting SharePoint lists to Excel. However, you should be aware that only SharePoint allows for data modification. Excel will update whenever you make changes to the SharePoint list, but not the other way around. If you attempt to change data in Excel, you won't receive an error warning; rather, upon refreshing, the data from SharePoint will replace your input.

- Select the Export to Excel button from the ribbon LIST tab in the SharePoint list.
- To enable the warning messages, click OK.
- In Excel, choose how you wish to see the data. Table, the default option, is frequently the most helpful. Excel will include and display every column from the SharePoint view that you export. Item Type and Path are two more columns that you will likely wish to conceal.

143

HOW TO USE EXCEL TO EXAMINE SHAREPOINT LIST DATA

After working with list items for some time, you will likely want to examine the data. You can examine data and create charts by exporting the list to Excel. SharePoint pages can also have Excel charts added to them; see Landing Page with Chart.

CHART AND PIVOT TABLE

By making a pivot table and a chart in Excel, you can examine data from a SharePoint list.

- Select "Summarize with PivotTable" from the ribbon DESIGN tab after clicking anywhere in the Excel table.

Summarize with PivotTable

- Decide whatever information you wish to see in the pivot table. The table you clicked in is the default choice.
- To work with any of the four pivot regions, drag and drop the fields you wish to use.
- Click the Pivot table and then the PivotChart button under the PIVOTTABLE TOOLS, ANALYZE tab to produce a chart.

144

- To view the data from the SharePoint list, pick your favorite chart style and design.

EXCEL DATA IMPORT/EXPORT DIRECTLY TO SHAREPOINT

There are numerous sharing benefits when Excel data is exported or imported into SharePoint. There are various methods for transferring data, and the key question is how much control and functionality you require. Is using Access worth the extra effort, or are the more straightforward direct export and import techniques covered in this section sufficient?

Although the two techniques listed below are fast, they have some significant disadvantages. Your data will be added to a new SharePoint list. Data is not pushed into an existing list by Excel. The new list's newly formed columns are List Columns rather than Site Columns. The Excel data can only be updated in SharePoint after it has been exported. The Excel Refresh option allows you to pull down changes from SharePoint to Excel, but not the other way around. Columns cannot be excluded from export or import, nor can their order be altered. The table or range will be moved exactly as it is. Columns cannot be excluded from export or import, nor can their order be altered. The list made from Excel data cannot be connected to Outlook using the method

145

outlined in Connect SharePoint to Outlook. A "clean up" of the SharePoint list can help with the additional issues with this approach of moving Excel data to SharePoint.

Use the Excel Export button to export an Excel table to a SharePoint list. Using Excel's "Export Table to SharePoint List" option to export an Excel table to a SharePoint list is the simplest method of transferring items between the two platforms.

- To get the new list generated, copy the URL to the SharePoint site. Keep in mind that you should only copy the website's URL: Create a table using the data in Excel.
- Select Export Table to SharePoint List after clicking the Export option under TABLE TOOLS >DESIGN >External Table Data.
- In the window that appears, paste the copied URL into the Address field.
- Select the read-only connection option.
- Type in the name you want to use for the next SharePoint list. You may also give it a description. Press Next.
- The many list columns that will be formed are shown in the newly opened dialog. Since nothing can be

146

changed here, you will need to go back and make adjustments in the table if the list appears incorrect. Press "Finish."

The information from the Excel table will now be put to a new SharePoint list that has been established on the website to which you provided the URL. You will receive a message dialog with a link to the updated list once the process is complete. The list can also be accessed by navigating to SharePoint Site Contents and finding it, or by clicking Excel's new Open in Browser button. Excel import into SharePoint

I demonstrated the process of exporting an Excel table to a SharePoint list above. Alternatively, you can use the Import Spreadsheet application to import the Excel table into SharePoint. Additionally, you can import a range of cells using that way without structuring them as a table.

- Install an app.
- Choose the Import Spreadsheet app after searching for Excel.

147

Import Spreadsheet

- Select the Excel file you wish to import and give the application a name.

- Type in the URL of the SharePoint website where the Excel table is to be imported.

- After selecting Import, you will be prompted to re-enter your SharePoint login credentials.

- Click Import after selecting the table or range you wish to import. The SharePoint list application will now import the Excel data you chose.

IMPROVE AN EXCEL EXPORT/IMPORT-CREATED SHAREPOINT LIST

Regretfully, not all SharePoint functionalities are utilized by the SharePoint list that is produced when an Excel table is exported or imported to a SharePoint list. The following advice may help you better adapt the new list to SharePoint:

- To view various iterations of the list, enable Version History.

- One of the main advantages of storing the data in SharePoint rather than Excel is this capability.

148

The new list's default view is Datasheet/Quick Edit rather than Standard view.

However, if you wish to display the list in a web component, using the Datasheet view by default causes issues. Thus, you may want to switch to Standard as the default view. See Edit Button and Data Entry View for information on adding an Edit button to the Standard view. Use Modify View to make the view clearer by excluding some columns. To display the data from various perspectives, create more views. See Edit Links to add the list to the Quick Launch.

THE WEB ACCESS WEB PART OF EXCEL

When displaying Excel content in SharePoint, the Excel Web Access web component comes in handy. This approach displays the Excel data in a web component rather than exporting it to SharePoint. This online section allows you to see the entire workbook or just a portion of it. Many choices are available in the Excel Web Access web component tool pane, primarily related to how the user interacts with the Excel content. I'll just cover the bare minimum here: how to specify which workbook and which section of that workbook should be shown in SharePoint.

- Go to Upload Files and add or save the Excel file to a SharePoint library.

149

- Select the page you wish to add Excel content to in Edit Mode.

- Include a Web element in the Business Data category, namely the Excel Web Access web element.

- Modify the Web Section.

- Click the Browse button to the right of the field to locate the Excel file, or type the Excel file's URL into the Workbook field in the web component panel.

- Click Apply and save the page if you wish to display the entire workbook.

- Choose the portion of the workbook you wish to display in Excel and give it a name. Then, before applying and saving, enter the name in the Named Item field in the web part panel. You can keep making changes to the Excel file using either the client version of Excel or Excel Online. Every time you save your modifications, the Excel Web Access web section will be updated.

LINK THE PROJECT AND SHAREPOINT

With its robust capabilities, Microsoft Project is a project management tool that assists managers in creating plans, allocating tasks, monitoring progress, controlling spending, and assessing workloads. Users without a project license or those who only require an overview of their activities and

150

the ability to mark them as finished as work progresses can share project tasks due to the fact that SharePoint can be utilized with Project. There is no automatic synchronization between Project and SharePoint. To update SharePoint with Project data and transfer any changes performed on the SharePoint side into Project (including live views, rights, and versions), click the Sync button in Project, regardless of whether you are creating new items in SharePoint or Project.

CONNECT THE SHAREPOINT TASKS LIST TO THE PROJECT FILE

Project can either construct a new SharePoint site with a tasks list if you start there, or you can first Create a SharePoint application based on the Tasks template and utilize it for the Project file.

- Open the file in Project and select Save as. Click on the "Sync with SharePoint" option.
- Make a brand-new website or provide the URL for an already-existing one. You can choose that URL from the list of sites if you have already synchronized a SharePoint site.
- Check the website.
- Click Save after selecting the list you wish to use. All of the Project items are now created in the Tasks

151

list, and connections between the Project and SharePoint fields have been made. The SharePoint Site Assets library is where the project file will be stored.

CONNECT THE PROJECT TO THE SHAREPOINT TASKS LIST

Project is used to see the data when you open a SharePoint tasks list in it. But everything is kept in SharePoint, including views and permissions. A SharePoint tasks list can be opened in Project in two ways:

- Click the Projects button under the ribbon LIST tab in the SharePoint list.

- Copy the SharePoint site's URL. Click the "New from SharePoint Tasks List" button in Project, then paste the URL. After that, choose the list you wish to open in Project by clicking the "Check Address" button.

A new project file will now be made, added to the SharePoint Site Assets, and linked to the SharePoint list.

152

LINK ACCESS AND SHAREPOINT

You can use Access tools like find and replace when you open a SharePoint list in Access, and copying and pasting is easier in Access than in the SharePoint datasheet view. Access can also be used as a bridge to link data from two platforms that aren't able to connect directly. For instance, you can link a SQL Server database to SharePoint or interact with SharePoint lists from other farms.

Additionally, you can use Access to export an Excel table to SharePoint. Compared to directly exporting or importing Excel data to SharePoint, this will allow you greater control over the connection.

SYNCHRONIZATION BETWEEN ACCESS AND SHAREPOINT

The SharePoint list and the generated Access table are synchronized when you open it in Access. Both SharePoint and Access allow for modification.

As soon as you switch to a new row in the Access table, the data you enter is saved to the SharePoint list. The linked Access table will be updated the next time it is opened or refreshed after you enter data in the SharePoint list.

HOW TO USE ACCESS TO OPEN A SHAREPOINT LIST

153

The "Open with Access" button under the LIST tab in the list ribbon will be activated if Internet Explorer determines that Access is installed on the PC. If so, click on it and choose "Link to data on the SharePoint site," which is the default setting. Since detection doesn't always work, you can open Access, make a new desktop database, and link it to the SharePoint list in this way if the button is inactive even though you have Access installed:

- Close the default table or remove it.
- Select SharePoint List by clicking the More button located beneath the EXTERNAL DATA tab in the ribbon.
- Paste or enter the URL of the website containing the list you wish to open in Access in the window that appears.
- Click Next after selecting the connected table option.
- All of the site's lists and libraries are now visible. It will open in a new table when you select the one you wish to utilize. Additionally, you can choose more than one list or library. They will all be linked together to form a linked table.

HOW TO USE ACCESS TO EXPORT AN EXCEL TABLE TO A SHAREPOINT LIST

154

I've demonstrated how to directly export and import Excel data to SharePoint above. You have more control over how data is added to the SharePoint list using the Access technique, despite it being more complex than the direct way:

- Which Excel columns you add to the SharePoint list is up to you. The distribution of data is up to you.
- You can import Excel data using an existing list that has Site Columns.

Both SharePoint and Access allow for modifications. Using the Access approach, you import an Excel datasheet and a SharePoint list into Access, where they appear as database tables. After that, you can write a query that transfers the desired data from the Excel file to the SharePoint table.

- Add the desired application type to SharePoint.
- Select "Open with Access" under the LIST tab; see Open a List in Access. A brand-new database is made. Choose the "Link to data on the SharePoint site" option.
- Locate the Excel file you wish to use in Access by clicking the Excel button under the EXTERNAL DATA tab. "Link to the data source by creating a linked table" is the option to choose.

155

- If there are headers in your Excel table, check the box for them.
- Give the new, connected table containing your Excel data a name.
- Select the Query Design button from the CREATE tab in Access.

- In the Query field, drag the Excel table.
- Select the Append button under the DESIGN tab.
- Click OK after choosing to append to the SharePoint list you have opened in Access.
- Double-click on the column names in the Query field of the Excel table.

After that, they will appear in the grid below for you to append. The column names can also be dropped into the grid by dragging and dropping them.

- Add the Excel columns to the SharePoint list's matching columns.
- Click the Run button under the DESIGN tab to execute the query.

You may now see the Excel data arranged in the list columns according to how you mapped it in Access when you return to the SharePoint list and refresh it.

This approach to using Access to import data into SharePoint is highly effective not only with Excel data sources but also with other data sources. See Import data from SQL to SharePoint Online below for an example using a SQL database.

REPEATED ACTIVITIES

I'll provide another example of updating SharePoint lists using Access queries in this section. A single Excel table serves as the starting point. This table lists the duties that must be completed on a monthly basis. The columns labeled "What," "Who," and "Day of Month" provide information about the tasks, the individuals assigned to them, and the deadlines.

Although there isn't a straightforward method for handling repeating activities in SharePoint, you can nevertheless make it simple to remember them and to confirm that they have been completed.

The challenge is to allow an Access query to update a SharePoint To Do Tasks list. When the tasks are finished, the

157

responsible parties can mark them as completed. Afterward, you can use SharePoint Alerts to remind them of the duties.

SHAREPOINT EXPORT

To obtain the data for recurring tasks in a SharePoint list, the first step is to export or import Excel data to SharePoint.

MAKE A LIST OF THINGS TO DO

Once the Excel data is in SharePoint, choose the Tasks list template and Add an App. I'll refer to this list as To-Do here. The What and Who information from Every Month list can now be copied and pasted into the To Do-list's Task Name and Assigned To fields. You must copy and paste recurring tasks for each month because the Due date column is more difficult to copy than the other columns.

Using a query to allow Microsoft Access manage the update is a better option. To have everything on the SharePoint To Do list, including the deadlines, you will then just need to execute the query once a month.

HOW TO USE AN ACCESS QUERY TO UPDATE THE TO DO LIST AFTER

Here, I'll walk you how to write a query that adds information from users' information and monthly SharePoint lists (imported from Excel) to a fresh SharePoint To Do list.

158

When you link Access to the SharePoint site, the UserInfo list—which is a secret SharePoint list—becomes visible. Even if you don't click the box, Access nonetheless generates a linked UserInfo table from the UserInfo list when you choose to utilize a list with an Assigned To field.

While the Who data cannot be immediately appended to the Assigned To field, the What field in the Every Month list can be directly appended to the Task name field in the To Do list. The UserInfo table must be used instead.

- Close the default table in Access and launch a blank desktop database.
- Click on More and choose SharePoint List under the EXTERNAL DATA tab. Use the Linked table option and provide the website's URL. Press the Next button.
- Examine the To Do and Every Month lists. When you click OK, the database will generate two new tables with the same names and contents as the lists. Additionally, a UserInfo table will be generated.
- Select the Query Design button from the CREATE tab. Choose the What and Who fields, then add Every Month table. (To add, click the Add button or double-click the field.)

159

- Select the Append button under the DESIGN tab. To the Task Name in the To Do database, append the What field from Every Month table.

- Either right-click in the query window and choose Show Table, or click the Show Table button under the DESIGN tab. Include the UserInfo table.

- Attach the UserInfo's ID to the Who field in Every Month table. You can add the Assigned To field, and this will appear in the query's second column.

- Choose Every Month table and click the Parameters button under the DESIGN tab to add the Due Date information to the To Do table as well.

- Type the month and year. They both ought to be integers.

- Select the DESIGN tab and click the Builder button.

- Choose Built-in Functions, Date/Time, Date Serial, and Functions.

160

- Choose the query you just prepared and the parameters Year and Month while you're still in the Builder.

- Choose the Day of Month and Every Month table for the current day. After selecting Value, select OK.

- The third query column will now include the expression you constructed. You can update "Expr1" to "Due Date" and add the Due Date field.

Field:	What	ID	Due: DateSerial(Year)
Table:	Every month	UserInfo	
Sort:			
Append To:	Task Name	Assigned To	Due Date

- To execute the query, select the Run button located beneath the DESIGN tab. The Year and Month parameters will now need you to input values. For both, use numbers.

- To update the SharePoint To Do list with all of the recurring tasks, run the query once a month and once a year.

161

CHAPTER TWELVE

HOW TO USE SQL TO IMPORT DATA INTO
SHAREPOINT ONLINE

It is not possible to directly enter data into a SharePoint list from a SQL Server database. Alternatively, you can use Access to open both the SharePoint list and the SQL Server database table. A query that transfers data from the SQL Server to SharePoint can then be created.

In this chapter, I'll explain how to add information to a SharePoint Online Contacts list from a contacts database table.

- Add a Contacts application to SharePoint.
- You can add or remove columns as you like.
- Go to Open a List in Access to access the Contacts list.
- Click the ODBC Database button in Access after selecting the EXTERNAL DATA tab from the ribbon.
- Click OK after selecting the radio choice labeled "Link to the data source by creating a linked table" in the window that appears.
- To create a new data source, utilize the SQL driver and click on New in the Select Data Source window.

162

- Keep the updated data source safe.

- To use the new data source, modify the default database.

- Choose the new data source and connect it to the Access table once you're back in the Select Data Source window.

- As the Unique Record, choose BusinessEntityID.

We can now link the SQL contacts database to the SharePoint contacts list, and we have two connections in Access: one with SQL and one with SharePoint. Now is the time to write a query that adds information to the SharePoint list by selecting it from the SQL database table.

- Select the SQL database table by clicking the Query Design button under the CREATE tab.

- To add data to the SharePoint list, click the Append button located beneath the ribbon DESIGN tab.

163

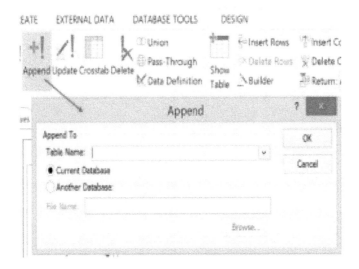

- Decide how to add the information from the SQL database table to the SharePoint list.
- To see the outcome, use the View button located beneath the ribbon DESIGN tab.
- Click the Save icon if everything appears to be in order.
- Click the Run button on the ribbon DESIGN tab to launch the query. The SharePoint list will now import the SQL Server data.

HOW TO LINK VISIO AND SHAREPOINT

Microsoft Office includes the schematization and vector graphics tool Visio. I've included two examples of how to utilize the Visio Access web component to show and interact with Visio drawings in SharePoint below. Additionally, SharePoint offers a site collection template designed for Visio files that comes with a default library.

THE WEB PART OF VISIO WEB ACCESS

Visio Web Access is a web component of Office Online that allows you to display Visio files. When displaying Visio content on a SharePoint page, this web component comes in handy.

USE VISIO WEB ACCESS TO ADD A VISIO DRAWING

Many choices are available in the Visio Web Access web component tool pane, primarily related to how the user interacts with the Visio material. I'll only go over the most fundamental here: how to specify which drawing should be shown in the online section.

- Go to Upload Files and add or save the Visio file to a SharePoint library.
- To add a Visio drawing, open the page in Edit Mode.
- Add a Web Part in the Business Data category. This is the Visio Web Access web part.
- Modify the Web Section.

165

- Either click the Browse button to the right of the field to locate the Visio file, or enter the URL to the Visio file in the Web Drawing URL field in the web component window.

- Customize the parameters for user interaction that you like.

- After selecting Apply, save the page.

As far as the settings permit, you can now manipulate the Visio drawing. However, keep in mind that you cannot click in the Visio Web Access web section and scroll the page because the drawing will then be in focus.

The Visio file that has been saved to SharePoint can still be updated. Every time you save your modifications, the Visio Web Access web section will be updated.

LINK VISIO WEB ACCESS TO A VISIO LIBRARY

To link a document library containing Visio files to the Visio Web Access web section, use a two-column page. In this manner, every file in the Visio library can appear on the same page in the Visio Web Access web section.

- Go to Upload Files and upload or save the Visio files you wish to show in SharePoint to a new document library.

166

- Add a page.
- Under the FORMAT TEXT tab, click the Text Layout button and choose the two columns option.
- Add the newly produced Visio files document library as a Web Part.
- Add a Web Part in the Business Data category. This is the Visio Web Access component.
- Modify the Visio Web Access Web Part.
- Choose Connections >Send Row of Data To >Visio Web Access after clicking the Edit arrow once more.
- Choose "Get Web Drawing URL" from the pop-up dialog.
- Select Configure.
- Link the Web Drawing URL field in the Consumer to the Document URL field in the Provider.
- Select "Finish," then "Apply" and "Save."

A drawing in the Visio drawing library web part can now be selected by clicking on its icon, and the drawing will be displayed in the Visio Web Access web part.

PROCESS REPOSITORY FOR VISIO

You will have a default document library that is tailored to Visio file sharing if you create a site collection for the Visio Process Repository. In addition to versioning and check-

167

Jason Taylor

in/check-out features, the default Visio Process Repository library includes columns that show validation status and cross-functional flowchart headers. Additionally, the collection offers a number of helpful flowchart and diagram templates.

- Establish a New Collection of Sites.
- Under the Enterprise tab, pick the Visio Process Repository site collection template.
- Click OK after making any more desired changes.

TASK AND TEMPLATES FOR THE ISSUE TRACKING LIST

The Tasks and Issue Tracking lists are two templates that SharePoint offers that can be used as helpdesk lists and frequently can be used in place of one another. Both offer advantages and disadvantages, and there are important distinctions to consider when choosing a list template. The only list with a timeframe is the **Tasks list**. Compared to the Issue tracking list, the Tasks list offers more built-in views.

There is no option to select what should be concealed; only the Tasks list item has a "Show more" link. When you open the Issue tracking list item, all fields are displayed. The "Start Date" column is only present in the Tasks list item. The only list item with a "Category" dropdown is the **Issue**

168

Tracking list item. There is only a Comments field on the Issue Tracking list item. The Tasks list item's "Predecessors" field corresponds to the Issue Tracking list item's "Related Issues" field. You lose the ability to synchronize the list with Outlook and Project if you use the Issues Tracking list template!

MAKE A LIST OF HELPDESKS

If a support staff should use the default SharePoint Issue Tracking list, I will offer some tips on what to consider and how to change it. Make a new list using the Tasks or Issue Tracking template. Next, alter the following:

- Edit the Quick Launch and move the list link to the permanent links once the list has been established and is visible under Recent. See Edit Links.

- To view various iterations of the list items, make sure versioning is enabled.

- Verify that the Assigned To column does not permit multiple selections by consulting Edit the Column.

- Instead of enabling multiple selection, add a new column for any additional individuals you wish to assign a job to.

169

- Modify the category names to reflect your team's preferences. The values should be written in alphabetical order.
- Go to Delete a Column to remove any columns you won't need, such the Related Issues column.

NOTICE BY E-MAIL TO ASSIGNED

Only SharePoint lists built on top of the Tasks or Issue Tracking template can use the E-mail Notification to Assigned alert. The person who has been given a task receives an automated email, and the setting is completed for the list rather than for the individual.

You can easily set up the Tasks and Issue Tracking email notice by just clicking a radio button, but there is no way to personalize the notification itself. Only after a job has been assigned to a user is it communicated to that user alone.

Although the email is often sent out a few minutes after the assignment, there is no control over when it is sent.

- Click on Advanced options under the General options group after opening the List Settings.
- Select "Send email when ownership is assigned" by clicking "Yes." Press OK.

170

You can design SharePoint Workflows to have more control over when emails should be delivered, what they should contain, and who should get them.

DATA ENTRY VIEW AND EDIT BUTTON

You want to get to the proper spot as fast as possible when you want to change existing data or add new information to a SharePoint list. You may streamline the process of entering data into a SharePoint list and reduce the number of clicks and waiting times by creating a Data Entry view or adding an edit button to an already-existing standard view.

THE EDIT BUTTON

You may rapidly enter edit mode for a single item without opening the entire list in edit mode when you add an edit button to a regular mode view.

- To add the Edit button, first open the list view.
- Adjust the View and select the "Edit (link to edit item)" Display checkbox.
- Choose the Edit button's first location. Press OK.

VIEW OF DATA ENTRY

When a Data Entry view is created, users who select that view are taken straight to a datasheet view. Naturally, you might as well select "edit this list," but when creating a new

171

item in a Data Entry view, you can also eliminate columns and retain only those that are important.

- To build a new view, first open the list.
- Choose the Datasheet View link after creating a view.
- Name the new view and add the personal touches you like.

EDIT MANY ITEMS IN A LIST

When you wish to make changes to multiple items on a list, instead of updating each one by hand, it is more convenient to do them all at once, particularly if they need to be altered consistently. Here, we'll examine methods for simultaneously editing several items in a SharePoint list.

- **Launch Edit Mode on the List.** You may now easily change values and drag the small handle in the bottom right corner of a cell, just like in Excel, to edit several items in the same way.
- **In Access, open a SharePoint list.** You can now edit many items that need to be modified in the same way by using Access's Find and Replace feature, and you can copy and paste faster than in SharePoint. Every

172

modification you make will be mirrored on the SharePoint site.

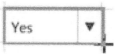

The quickest way to change multiple items in a SharePoint list that is open in Access is to run a query:

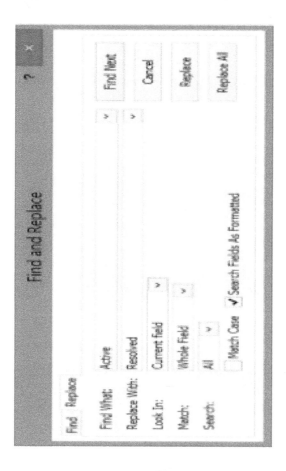

173

- Click the Query Design button under the CREATE tab in the Access ribbon.
- Add the list table to the query.

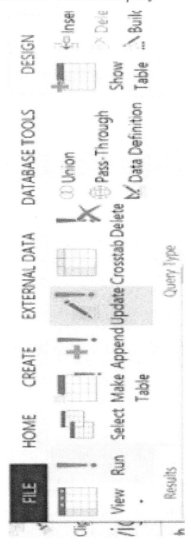

174

- Click the Update button under the DESIGN tab in the ribbon.
- Choose the field that needs to be updated.
- Enter the update value and the criteria.
- Click the Run button under the DESIGN tab in the ribbon. At this point, the values will be rapidly changed and everything will be reflected back to the SharePoint site.

175

CHAPTER THIRTEEN

PHONE CONTACTS

I'll demonstrate how to utilize SharePoint to automate phone message delivery inside a company in this chapter. Additionally, the system allows users to indicate whether or not the phone message has been handled.

Going through all this bother for phone messages may seem a bit excessive, but my goal is to reiterate and broaden strategies that we have already discussed and that you can apply to any information delivery inside your company. Everyone can relate to the straightforward facts in the phone texts.

I will start by outlining a straightforward solution that is challenging to scale. After that, I'll demonstrate a more sophisticated method that can be used across numerous site collections within a SharePoint tenant.

COMPILE A LIST OF PHONE MESSAGES

I'll start this section by going over how to make a basic SharePoint list application for phone messages that can accommodate a small business or a small user base. I will then demonstrate a more sophisticated method that can be used across numerous site collections within a SharePoint tenant.

BASIC LIST

Since List Columns were used to generate the simple list, it cannot be reused.

- Include the Custom List app.
- In the Quick Launch, the list will appear under Recent. Drag the updated list out of Recent after selecting EDIT LINKS.)
- Access the List Preferences.
- Open the Title column and change its name to a different one-line text field, like "Caller phone number."
- Create List Columns: a Yes/No column for Returned, with the default value set to No; a People or Group column for the called individual; and a single line of text column for Caller name.

There are two options besides making the list from scratch if you wish to utilize the same type of list on another website:

- You can save the app as a template and use it for the new list if it's part of the same site collection.
- You can upload the template to another site collection once the updated list is in that collection.

177

BUSINESS LIST

You must first build a content type in The Content Type Hub using Site Columns in order to generate a list that can be utilized throughout the SharePoint tenant. After that, you can link the content type to a list you've created in the Content Type Hub.

The views are not provided by the content type, but it does provide the columns and properties you want to utilize for each list item. In order to save the list as a template, you should first construct the views you require.

The template may then be used to build new lists with the same content type and views in all site collections with the same settings. (You may still utilize the content type and just add the views for site collections with different parameters.)

ESTABLISH A CONTENT TYPE FOR PHONE MESSAGES

- Launch the Hub for Content Types.
- Establish a Type of Content.

178

- Use the item in the List Content Types group as the basis for the new content type.

Parent Content Type:

Select parent content type from:

| List Content Types | ∨ |

Parent Content Type:

| Item | ∨ |

Description:
Create a new list item.

- Add the content type to a group of content types, either new or existing.
- Press OK.
- For each content category, create a new Site Column and add it to the same new Site Column group.

Keep in mind that changing the Title field to "phone number," like we did when we created the list column above, would change the Title fields in every tenant content type! You can publish the content type to make it accessible to the entire tenant once the columns have been generated.

MAKE A LIST OF PHONE MESSAGES ASSOCIATED WITH A TYPE OF CONTENT

- In the Content Type Hub, add an application called Custom List.

179

- Link the Phone Messages content type to the newly created Custom List; see Connect the Content Type to an App.

- Remove the default type of content.

VIEWS OF PHONE MESSAGES

For a list of phone messages, I recommend four views:

- Calls made today,
- Calls sorted by caller
- Calls that were not returned, and lastly,
- An entry view.

For general information on creating views, see Create a View. I will just discuss what makes each list unique here. Group by the Called column for the Grouped View. Only things where the Returned value is not equal to Yes should be displayed in the un-returned calls view once the items have been filtered by the Returned column. (This is a safer option than choosing "no."

ENTRY VIEW

It will be quite simple to enter new messages if you construct an Entry view based on the Datasheet view type.

180

- Choose the Datasheet view type and conceal the Returned column to generate this view. (Calls entered in this list have not yet received a response.)
- To display only objects with the ID 0, filter the items. No current items will be displayed in this view since there aren't any such objects. Only fresh phone messages should be entered using it.

- Choose the Datasheet view type and conceal the Returned column to generate this view. (Calls entered in this list have not yet received a response.)
- To display only objects with the ID 0, filter the items. No current items will be displayed in this view since there aren't any such objects. Only fresh phone messages should be entered using it.

VIEW OF TODAY'S CALLS

To see only things created today, use the Today's view filter and the Standard view type.

181

- To choose the current day as the filter, type [Today].

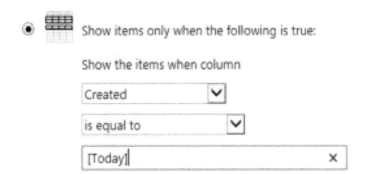

WORKFLOW ALERT PHONE MESSAGES

I'll demonstrate two different email alert routines for missed calls in this section. One is appropriate for the basic phone message SharePoint list app. When your list of phone messages is based on a content type in the Content Type Hub, I advise you to utilize the alternative workflow since it is reusable and can be linked to a content type.

The caller's name, phone number, and information about who answered the call should all be included in the message. Having a link to the list item in edit mode is also beneficial because it allows the user to mark the call as returned fast.

ONE LIST WORKFLOW

182

Although the one list workflow's phases are designed for a SharePoint workflow, a SharePoint workflow can also be used. Although the procedures differ slightly, the primary distinction is that the SharePoint workflow must be terminated. The other acts are comparable.

- Launch SharePoint Designer and open the site.
- To view the summary page for the Phone Messages list, navigate to Lists and Libraries and click on it.
- Get a list workflow started. Configure the process to begin automatically upon creation of an item. It can also be configured to start manually.
- Type "go" and hit Enter at the "Transition to Stage" screen. Choose End of Workflow after clicking on the stage.
- Choose the "Send an Email" action.
- Choose a Workflow Lookup for a User after clicking on "these users."
- Choose the "Email Address" return field and the "Called" field from the source.
- Type in the email's subject line and body. The lookups you wish to use should be added.
- Check and publish the workflow.

A lookup for the name of the caller in the subject line is appropriate. You can include lookups for the recipient's phone number, creation time, and email address in the body of the message.

ADD AN ITEM LINK IN THE EMAIL WORKFLOW

You should first copy the link to one of the items and then construct a lookup for the ID if you want the email message that the workflow sends to include a link to the list item from which the email information was collected. This type of link allows the recipient of the email to mark the call as returned and open the list item straight from the email.

- Click the Edit Item button after selecting one of the existing items in the SharePoint Phone Messages list.
- Choose Properties with a right-click on the form.
- In edit mode, copy the item's path.
- If the Phone Messages workflow isn't open in SharePoint Designer, click on Workflows and locate it.
- To view the email message, click the "Current Item Called" link.
- Include a display text in the body of the email and choose it.

184

- Select the String Builder button after selecting the Edit Hyperlink button.

- In the String Builder, paste the copied link.

- Click the "Add or Change Lookup" button after selecting the ID number from the link.

- Choose the ID from the source in the field.

- Select OK in every dialog box, then publish and verify the workflow.

WORKFLOW REUSABILITY

A reusable SharePoint process can be used in any list that contains the Phone Message content type if it is created and connected to it. But in order to use it, you need to save it as a template and upload it to each site collection. The same lookups and actions as in the list workflow above can be used. Additionally, take note that SharePoint Designer does not specify the workflow's execution time. This is carried out for reusable workflows at the site collection level.

- Begin developing a workflow that can be reused.

- Choose to build a SharePoint workflow and give the process a name.

- Click OK after connecting the workflow to the Phone Message content type.

185

- Construct the process according to the prior section's instructions for the list workflow.

MY CONTACTS

A frequently visited website, like the SharePoint home page, can have a Content Search web component added that displays each user's phone messages. This example displays the current user's unanswered calls regardless of the site collection in which the phone messages were generated.

- Go to Edit Mode and open a page.
- Under the FORMAT TEXT tab, click the Text Layout button and choose "One column with sidebar." This will display a web component in the sidebar with the default document library.
- We will add the web part for the unreturned calls here, therefore delete the default web part.
- Include the Content Rollup category's Content Search web component.
- The most recent modified entries in the site collection are displayed by default in the web section. Edit the Web Part and use the "Change query" option to make that change.

186

- Choose "Items matching a content type" in the Query Builder, without restricting by app. Limit the search to the content type of phone messages.
- Go to Advanced Mode and add two property filters: "CallereturnedOWSBOOL" "Not equals" and "CalledOWSUSER" "Contains" "The name of the user who runs the query." manually, and the answer is in the affirmative.
- Adjust any further web part settings you like, then save the page.

IMPROVEMENTS

You can improve the phone messages solution further by, for instance, adding a Managed Metadata column to the phone messages list and a phone messages search vertical in the Search Center. Since Managed Metadata and search verticals have already been covered in this book, I will merely highlight the unique features of the phone messaging application here.

MAKE A VERTICAL SEARCH FOR PHONE MESSAGES

You can locate these messages faster if you add a Search Vertical to the Search Center that is limited to the phone messages content type. For instance, you can display the

187

caller's name on the first line and the phone number on the second line of every item you find if you want to display the search results in a custom results web part.

I advise you to alter the page's refinement web section when you make a search vertical page. Add refiners that are useful in a search and eliminate those that aren't.

OVERSIGHT OF METADATA

You will have more information without adding more columns for users to fill out if you add a Managed Metadata column to the list of phone messages and specify the Default Column Values.

Don't set a default value when using a content type; instead, edit the content type and add a Managed Metadata column.

Instead, you should open the column in each list where the content type is used and set the default value there after republishing and the customary delay. In this manner, you can choose the default value that works best for every list.

RENTAL CONTRACTS

Rental agreements serve as the foundation for this chapter. Contract renewals must be handled promptly, and they must be registered in a way that provides a clear picture of what the organization is renting.

My goal is not to provide a formula for developing the ideal rental agreement management tool. Rather, I would want to highlight a few approaches that may be helpful when you deal with comparable information sharing scenarios in your own company.

In order to make it simple to construct lists of the same kind using Add an app, we will first establish a content type with appropriate site columns, link it to a list, and then create a template from the list.

Additionally, two reusable workflows will be developed: one that establishes the renewal date and another that notifies the person in charge of the renewal via email. Lastly, we will establish two retention policies: one for the email workflow and another for the duration of rental agreements.

TYPE OF CONTENT

Creating a Content Type for the rental agreements lists is the first step in developing a solution for rental agreements. If you want the entire tenant to have access to it, create it from The Content Type Hub; if you want to utilize it in only one collection, create it from the root site of a Site Collection.

Choose the content type based on the item and the List Content Types group. You can utilize the Title column to enter the name of the rented place in the list that results.

189

I recommend the columns listed below. Don't take my remarks concerning new or current site columns too literally; they are based on what most organizations already have or don't have. The area in square meters of the hired space: a new site column of the Number type.

The leasing agreement's start date is listed in an existing site column. The leasing agreement's expiration date is listed in an existing site column. An existing site column is the department renting the space. Renewal Date: a new Date and Time-type site column. A new site column with the Person or Group type designates the person responsible for the rental agreement.

Following the creation of the content type, Add a Custom List and an App, then link the list to the content type of the rental agreement.

TEMPLATE

Include your preferred views and settings in the list of rental agreements. In addition to opening the form in a new dialog and having an edit button visible, I advise you to enable version history. Save the rental agreement list as a template once you have a good list. It will appear among the other templates for SharePoint apps, and using one of these

190

templates makes it simple to make new lists for different types of rental agreements.

Naturally, you can have all of the rental agreements in one list as well, but if you have several lists, you can provide each one a distinct set of rights, and users won't be overloaded with stuff from one list.

WORKFLOW FOR THE RENEWAL DATE

The renewal date will be set to two months prior to the rental agreement's expiration date using a repeatable workflow that we will design here. Begin developing a workflow that can be reused. Link the rental agreements content type to the workflow.

- Set the Renewal Date to "is less than" 1971 or another unattainable value, and choose the Condition to "If current item field equals value." The key takeaway here is that users should leave the field empty, which would provide a field value below 1971.

- Choose the "Add Time to Date" Action and enter "End Date" for the Date and "-2 months" for the Time. To a new variable, output.

- Choose the Action "Update List Item" and enter the new variable's value in the Field Renewal Date.

191

- Check and publish the workflow.

Assign a Content Type to the Reusable Workflow; in this example, the content type for rental agreements. For the entire site collection, that is completed once. The renewal date workflow will then be present in all listings that employ the rental agreements content type.

WORKFLOW FOR RENEWAL E-MAIL

We developed a reusable workflow in the section above that adjusts the rental agreement renewal date to two months prior to the agreement's expiration date. Here, we will develop a reusable procedure that sends a renewal reminder to the responsible party, who should receive an email about the renewal on the day of the renewal.

- Begin developing a workflow that can be reused.
- Choose the "Send an Email" action.
- Set a Workflow Lookup for a User to the Responsible Person in the e-mail To field, then return the result as an email address.
- Enter the text you like to use in the String Builder for the email Subject box. Then, add a lookup for the Title, which is used to represent the location's name.
- Type or paste the material you wish to use in the email body. (For instance, as shown in the image

192

below, you can make a table in Word, paste it in the body field, and then add lookups for the values of the current item in the content type columns.)

- Include a link in the item of the rental agreement. From the function guide, select the link. Select the field from source "Current Item URL" and the data source "Workflow Context."

- Check and publish the workflow.

Connect the Reusable Workflow to a Content Type that appears in the lists of rental agreements. For the entire site collection, that is completed once. The send renewal e-mail procedure will thereafter be available for any lists that employ the rental agreements content type.

NOTE: This process is still ongoing. Every rental agreement must be established to begin on a particular date. See the following section, Retention Stages, for the definition of this date in the Information Management Policy Settings.

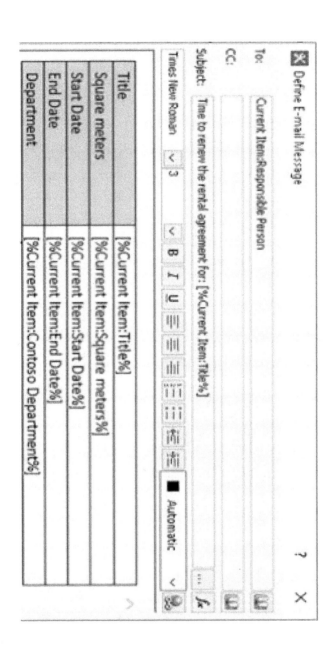

STAGES OF RETENTION

You must construct a retention stage in the content type's Information Management Policy Settings in order to configure the email sending date for the Renewal E-mail Workflow, which was built in the section above. In addition to setting the rental agreements to be permanently erased at a predetermined number of years following the expiration date, you can also arrange the alarm to be sent on a calculated date.

- From the site collection's root site, access the Site Settings.

- Click on the 'Site content types' option in the Web Designer Galleries group.

- Choose the content type itself after selecting the content type group that includes the rental agreements content type.

- Select the option labeled "Information management policy settings."

- To add two retentions, enable retention and select "Add retentions stage." Set the Event Renewal Date to 0 days and select "Action" to initiate the workflow that generates the renewal alert.

195

Choose the Action to Delete the item permanently and the Event End Date to the number of years you want. You may verify that these retention settings are active in a list by going into the List settings and selecting the "Information management policy settings" link, but you cannot check them right away because they depend on time. A notification stating that the policy settings are inherited from the parent content type and cannot be altered should appear when you click on the content type.

196

CONCLUSION

In this tutorial book, we have delved deeply into the multifaceted features and functionalities of SharePoint, equipping you with the skills and knowledge needed to effectively utilize this powerful platform. From the foundational aspects of setting up your SharePoint environment to the intricacies of customizing workflows, managing content, and enhancing collaboration, you now possess a comprehensive understanding of how to leverage SharePoint to improve productivity and teamwork within your organization.

Throughout this journey, we've covered a wide array of topics, including:

Site Creation and Management: You've learned how to create and manage sites tailored to your organization's needs, ensuring that all team members have access to the resources they require.

Document Management: We explored best practices for document storage, version control, and sharing, helping you maintain an organized and efficient document library.

Collaboration Tools: By examining features such as lists, libraries, and team sites, you now understand how to foster

197

collaboration among team members, regardless of their physical location.

Workflows and Automation: You've gained insights into automating processes with Power Automate, allowing you to streamline repetitive tasks and enhance overall efficiency.

Security and Permissions: We emphasized the importance of security within SharePoint, guiding you on how to manage permissions and protect sensitive information.

As you move forward in your SharePoint journey, it's essential to recognize that learning is an ongoing process. SharePoint is a dynamic platform that continually evolves, with Microsoft frequently introducing new features and updates aimed at enhancing user experience and functionality. To stay ahead of the curve, consider engaging with the SharePoint community through forums, webinars, and online courses. These resources can provide valuable insights, tips, and best practices that will help you maximize the platform's capabilities.

Additionally, keep an eye on emerging trends in collaboration technology. As remote work becomes increasingly prevalent, understanding how SharePoint integrates with other tools and platforms will be crucial for leveraging its potential fully. Whether it's integrating with

198

Microsoft Teams, utilizing Power Apps for custom solutions, or exploring advanced analytics with Power BI, the possibilities are vast.

Finally, we hope this book has empowered you with the knowledge and practical skills necessary to make the most of SharePoint. By implementing the strategies and techniques outlined in these chapters, you can transform how your organization collaborates, manages information, and drives productivity. Embrace the possibilities that lie ahead, and continue to explore and innovate within the SharePoint ecosystem. Happy SharePointing!

www.ingramcontent.com/pod-product-compliance
Lightning Source LLC
LaVergne TN
LVHW022343060326
832902LV00022B/4210